POL___ FROM A RUNAWAY

A TRUE STORY
BY
BEN WESTWOOD

Written and published by
Ben Westwood.
© 2017

www.benwestwooduk.blogspot.co.uk

Parental guidance advised.
Not suitable for young children.

Cover illustration and design by
Neil Paterson
www.lynniel.com

I dedicate this book to Sylvie, the first to shine a light on a great love that only a parent could understand.

To Mum, for the crap I put her through, and giving up her youth to bring me into this world.

To Dad and Kirsty for their great support and encouragement, especially throughout this project.

To all my friends and family, past foster parents, social workers and children's home staff that made a positive impact on my life.

To all the young people in care, care leavers and those working with them.

To the Connection at St Martins, for being my saving grace both as a runaway and immediately afterwards as a young homeless adult.

And to the whole world.
Pick up the phone and call that person no-one has a clue what is doing.

Let go of your grudges.
There is strength in forgiveness.
There is treasure in love.

CONTENTS

INTRODUCTION

Plenty of people I've met that have heard snippets of my life story often comment about how hard it must have been.

The truth is, during most of this adventure, it wasn't. Not consciously anyway.

As you'll find out, things certainly could have turned out much worse for me.
A lot of the people I'd met on the streets had stories a lot more heartbreaking than mine.

And fortunately for me, some of the folk in this book were an important part in changing my outlook on life. I sometimes wonder - who or what I could have become without these kinds of moments.

For those that don't know me (and those that perhaps think they do!), I don't do the streets anymore.

Sure I've had my times being homeless as an adult, and perhaps with stories like this comes other hurdles, but being the sort of young person I was, it often felt easy.

I guess that I've softened up a bit now in my adult life.

But it wasn't until the age of thirty-two – whilst writing this book – that I've ever really reflected on my teenage years as a whole. It's been somewhat strengthening.

A lot of the people that I've written about in this book are now in a completely different time and space. Some for better and some for worse, but for most part – they've learned their wisdom along the way.

Perhaps this book will help refresh people's memories into some of the abstract choices that can be made by a child's mind?

Or perhaps give one or two social workers a better understanding of bamboozling work cases such as I was?

Welcome to my teenage world of runaways, drug-addicts, predators, alcoholics, prostitutes, down-and-outs, bag ladies, angelic acquaintances and beautiful souls.

Just one more thing…

Donations and money can only do so much for people. If you really want to help the soul of a homeless person, share with them a setting that you yourself would enjoy too..

Share dinner with them, get to know them, invite them to a party, play a game with them, invite them to football or do something creative…
Just connect.

The real deal.
Some may have no idea of its importance.

So without further ado, I present to you, my childhood.

1984

It all started, one night around late September, 1984.
On a mattress in a squat, apparently.

Punks and Skinheads, only young. Mum was sixteen, my
dad eighteen, and on that night of late September, she
fell pregnant, with me.

I grew in her throughout the new year into 1985, right
up into the summer month of July, where I'd been
slightly resistant to come out - but eventually did.

From some point during those nine months inside her,
well, I guess I'd always been destined to have an uncertain
future. Luckily in the end I never was put up for
adoption, and my mum decided to give up her own youth
instead, to raise me.

My earliest memory (I think) was of being upside down in
a Ford Capri with my mum alongside me, asking if I was

alright. Then being helped out of the car by the man I
presumed was driving it.

Second to that, for my first seven or so years, had been
a memory of a man in a black bomber jacket taking me
out to buy sweets. He'd often pop into my head he would.

The black-and-white TV on, and mum crying. The Tories
had got in again. I didn't understand it, but it seemed to
upset her a lot.
Both of us hiding behind the sofa.
The taxman outside knocking at the door.
And my Roland Rat.

Going to nursery and getting bitten on the arm.
Sitting on tractor tyres on the playground.
And the phone box outside of our house.

When I'd been around four, we moved away, not that far,
with my mum's new boyfriend a few miles down the road,
to nearby Rugeley.

A once bustling mining town before the pits had closed
down, but had become somewhat declining by the time we'd

moved there.

Frank Gee Close. Sitting on cheap skateboards and
rolling down the hill.
Hitting the wall at the bottom.

Making dens with old bits of thrown out house interior.
At six, being jumped by a group of twelve year olds that
had stamped on my arm and broken it.

And Olly Owl, whom they also had stitched and bandaged
up for me when I came out of theatre and onto the
children's ward.

Wearing the flaky cheap cast I'd worn for six weeks.
Getting it cut off and finding old bits of pizza.
The guy I called dad organising fights with older boys in
the street, in an attempt to toughen me up.

Not really having any interest in wanting to hit them
back, though after a punch in the face and a short delay,
I would.

Mum sending me off to the old ladies house at the top
of the hill, to help her with her chores.
Lovely old gal, ever so sweet.

Being out in the sea in a rubber dingy with mum and 'dad', mum screaming to get more inland because it was scaring her being out that far, and just about seeing the beach on the horizon.

'Dad' driving us at high speed towards a tree saying that we were all going to die, only to brake suddenly at the very last moment inches away from it.

Having a crush on Gemma across the street.
Giving her my Walkman.
Writing some crazy story about her dad fighting off a big dragon.

Wishing I'd had a proper plastic sled for the hill when it snowed in the winter.
Sliding down on a bin bag, and hurting my arse.

A drunken neighbour throwing a brick through my bedroom window whilst standing outside swaying.
My MDF 'cabin' bed.

My sister being born.
The bangs, and violent sounding arguments.

Being in cars with mum late at night, unsure of where
we were going before heading back home a few days later.
More loud noises coming from upstairs.
It's fighting again.

Me hovering at the top of the stairs, trying to make out
exactly what was happening.
Holding my sister whilst sitting downstairs she'd only
been a few months old. Talking to her, to try and drown
out the noise from above.

Running into their room with a cricket bat yelling at
'dad' to leave her alone.
Him chasing me out. Really, what could I do?

My brother being born.

By now I was around seven or eight.
As far as I'd been told, he was my dad.
But I was confused.
Nothing could stop the memory of the man in the black
bomber jacket with the orange inside lining.
Why did I always have the same vision of him walking
towards me, like a spirit living in my head?
I can't quite make out the face.

But there's something about him.

More fighting, and then mum's friend Elaine came round.
And that's when I said it, without really thinking,
"He's not my real dad is he?"
She seemed shocked, looking at Elaine unsure of how to
reply. Parenthood ay.

Fair play to her though, she said I was right, and when I
was a little older that she'd tell me everything I wanted
to know, about who my real father was.

Not too long after, we'd moved down the road to a council
estate called the Springfields, locally known as 'The
Springies'.

All the streets went around in squares, and all named
after famous folk.
William Morris Court was where we lived.
Kwik-Save right across the road, pretty handy, and
there became home.

SPRINGFIELDS

They've split up for good.
New place, it seems nice.
A fresh start.

On the first day of moving in, I'm invited by one of the
other kids in the street to play out, and so from there I
meet the others.
Hide and seek.

My first kiss.
With a girl three years older than me called Katherine,
in the shed.

Mum going out, now it's me babysitting.
I'm the eldest, so I help mum out a little.
Her coming back late, merry, seeming free.
I'm happy for her, it's nice to see her out enjoying
herself these days. A release.

For a short while she's dating a guy, a few years
younger, seems a nice fella, a good soul.

Mum's Amiga A500 plus.
Trays full of floppy disks with all sorts of crazy games.
Sensible soccer.
Supporting Arsenal simply because I'd often be them on that game.

Playing WWF with my mates, jumping off furniture and getting each other into submission moves.
Letting my schoolmates draw the ultimate warrior mask on my face with a biro, and telling my mum that they had all forced me into it.
Moving primary school mainly because of that.

Being a weird kid, jumping on tables, odd behaviour.
Stealing from the tuck-shop regularly after break times, and being the sole purpose of it being closed down.

Being invited out to play football by my older neighbour called Bertie, from a couple of doors away, mainly because he had no-one else to go in goal to practise his shooting at.

Dodging a ball, travelling at the speed of light and hearing it slam from the sound of the fence behind me.

Before long all the boys and girls are in teams for a
match.
And unlike at first, I now love being in goal.
Getting called in by our mum's for dinner.
Playing until we could hardly see the ball.

Mum struggling, stressed, breaking down.
But all three of us, always fed and clothed.
Power rangers, I'd loved it from the start.
Took the world by storm.

Etching Hill primary, but I still haven't ventured much
further past the other side of the school, where the
kids that lived in the big houses and had the cool toys
were, by the big stone Hill.

Being given two 'pogs' and a 'slammer' from a friend in
school. Started beating everyone.
The kid that was used to being 'pog champion' crying
when I'd completely wiped him out.

'If it affects you that much mate, have um back.'
Doing a sixties play and becoming obsessed with the
Beatles, John Lennon in particular.
Getting a Beatles bowl cut, for a little while.

Falling in love with football.
Passionate goalkeeper.
When no-one was out I'd kick a ball against a wall to
try and catch it.
Loved it.

Discovering money in the teacher's draws after being
told I could collect my pogs from there after lessons.
Telling the cleaners that I was collecting my pogs.
Stealing money. A regular habit.

Buying sweets and toys, and telling my mum that my
friend's parents had been giving them to me, when she'd
ask where they were from.
The teachers eventually sussing me out, and asking my
mum to come in for a chat.

Two and two were put together.
Mum having words with me. Definitely grounded.
Beforehand, she thought that I might have been
groomed.

Wearing my Borussia Dortmund charity shop 'BVB'
hoody with the big pouch.
Great for pinching sweets and that.

Mum meeting a new bloke, he used to be in the army.
Sometimes he comes, and we all play monopoly.
He seems alright. And then he moves in.

He's made an effort, and taken me fishing and shooting
with him.

Perhaps it had been more obvious than I'd realised myself,
but it just probably weren't my sort of thing.
Not something I had ached to do that soon again.

Playing football with the older lads over on Kwik-Save
car park.
Most of them growing-up.

Soon another crew of us would form, and play on the
grass at the other side.
Jumpers for goalposts, crazy goal celebrations.
Bull-shitting to my mates that I played for Arsenal
under-sixteens.

Knocking on their doors at the weekend for them to ask
me why I'm not in London to play against the QPR
youth team, like I said I was going to be.
"Oh it's cancelled" was often my excuse.

Being asked to go to Kwik Save with my brother and sister. Nicking a big chocolate bar, thinking that they were both too young to understand what was happening. My sister grassing me up to mum.

Not got a father figure mum had felt, perhaps eventually her new boyfriend could help inspire some discipline in me.

Sunday lunches. Walking ten minutes to the local Spar for apple sauce, before they'd closed at two in the afternoon.

The smell of cooking from everyone's houses, whilst walking on the way there and back.
Doing all the washing up afterwards.
I'd always hated doing all the big pans and everything, but nevertheless, it was my job to do.

Her new fella shining it all up to the light, to check if I'd done it properly.
If there's any marks on anything again, he'll put everything I've done back into the sink.
Repeated situations.
Me calling him a bully, and telling him to fuck off.

My discipline for that, was one that had come from the army.

An awkward relationship between us had occurred.

Them needing space, I was out into the wild I guess.
Lonely weekends, no-one plays football so much anymore.
My friends are all out with their folks, what to do.

Rainy days sheltering under the supermarket cladding.
Making prank calls to the operator in the nearby phone boxes.

Calling Childline with a false story, not wanting them to do anything or feel sorry, but just to pass the time.
Ordering taxi's and pizza's to people houses.
Once in a while it was the fire brigade.

Meeting up with other wanderers, and another lad around my age,
Smoking, and coughing.

Deciding to run away, in the spur of the moment, with a ten-pound note my mum had given me to go to the chip shop with, just after it had snowed.

Arriving back to the porch later on that evening, too worried to knock the door. So I waited until mum had found me.
I'm definitely grounded.

And then came high school, and being one of the youngest in my year - I was eleven.

Instead of going to the school closest which most of the kids from our estate had gone to, my mum thought it best I went to the one across the other side of town, as her fella had gone there and had gave it his approval.

Truanting and running around the school during lessons, both on my own and with others.
A common occurrence.

On my next warning, I would be to get a written notice to my mum and a week's suspension.

GREAT HAYWOOD

Another bad letter from school today,
And my mum has already got stress.
I just feel now that I'm a burden on people,
And this is just gonna make mess.

Don't wanna hear anger, don't wanna hear shouting,
And I don't wanna make my mum swear.
I just feel it's better for everyone here,
If I made my own way elsewhere.

I don't really know where I'm going,
But the road down to Stafford ain't far.
I just really hope, that I don't get caught,
By someone that spots me from a car.

So I make my way, a mile and half down the road,
Until there's a turning to take.
There's a sign that says 'Stone' and the name sounds
quite cool,
So that is the way that I make.

Never heard of this place, but I think with that name,
that there's surely something to see.
So I head on my way, and I think by now,
That my mum could be looking for me.

I walk through the village of Little Haywood,
Still trying to head towards Stone.
Across the road were two girls, and one recognised me,
And I told them I'd ran off from home.

They offered to help me get somewhere to sleep,
"We'll sneak you some food too", they said.
I met them both later, and at first the plan,
Was for one of them to sneak me into their shed.

"I can't get you in, because my dad is at home,
But here's a blanket you can keep.
I know just the place, there's a ditch down the road,
It's sheltered and you'll get some sleep"

So we made our way and walked up the road,
Through the village and then to the top end.
We then get to a junction, where there's a main road,
the way to Stone just round the bend.

One girl pointed over to across the road,

And said "Look there's that ditch you can stay.
It's covered in trees, look we got to go back,
Because there's not much light left in the day."

They'd gave me a pillow and I made a bed,
With a blanket and a bag that I'd lent.
They gave me some fruit and said "We've got to scoot,
We'll see you tomorrow" then went.

I wondered around for a short while,
But soon did come the dark night.
And every few minutes came fast cars and headlights,
And I just hoped that I'd stayed out of sight.

By now I know, that I've crossed the line,
And I've actually now ran away.
But I'm under the moon and now look at the stars,
And haven't thought once about the next day.

When morning came, I then wandered around,
But there's nothing at all here I can do.
So I waited around, to meet up with the girls,
When I'll see them next I've not got a clue.
In the afternoon I then bumped into them,

When they had got back home from their school.
"The police have been asking everyone about you"
She said, but I just kept my cool.

"We'll pop up by later, and drop you some food",
One of the girls had then said to me.
"I'll sneak out my pudding, and come and bring it out, to
you once I've finished my tea".

I met them both later and one girl had said,
"Maybe it's time that you went back home."
I said "I'll be alright, I'll just stay one more night,
Then make my way over to Stone."

And then around midnight I must have been tired,
As I stared at the branch of a tree.
For over five minutes, I'd contemplated,
If there was a big spider in front of me.

I'd got really scared and then so made a leap,
Right out of the bush quick like a stag.
Now what do I do? Because in there's my blanket,
My food, my coat and my bag.

So I make my way just a few yards down the road,
To a house with some lights I could see.
I knocked on the door, a middle-aged man had then
answered,
I said "Please mate, could you help me?"

"I think there's a spider in the bush I've been sleeping,
And I just need to get back my stuff."
"How old are you mate?" he then asked me,
"And why are you out there sleeping rough?"

"Seventeen" I replied, and I've been kicked out,
Is there anything at all you can do?"
"I'll just get my torch" he then said in reply,
"Then I will come there to help you."

We walked to the bush and then he shone his torch,
And said "Mate, there's nothing to fear,
Your stuff is alright, and there is no sight,
Of a spider that would bite you here."

So then I said "Thanks", and then off the man went,
And I felt like a fool for my scare.
And then I could see around four miles away,
A helicopter up in the air.

"What if that helicopter was looking for me?
"It's probably not" in my head I had said.
Before closing my eyes, to try to get some sleep,
But I still have those thoughts in my head.

I'd got no more than around one hour of sleep,
And I'd woken up covered in sticks.
I went to find warmth, but there was nowhere at all,
By now it was sometime around six.

Two hours go by, oh now what should I do?
I shouldn't stay here one day again.
But most of my morning I simply spent trying,
To get myself out of the rain.

I did all that I could, to try and find shelter,
But there's nowhere, this village is small.
And then on my way back, again to the ditch,
It seemed that I'd hit a brick wall.

I don't know how I'm gonna survive,
No money, no food and I'm wet.
There's nowhere to go, except for back home,
And then I found myself upset.

The only thing, I could think of to do,
Was to flag down a car that came by.
And tell them that I, have ran away,
Maybe they'll get me home into the dry.

So I see some cars, and I wave and I shout,
But the first five cars ignore.
And then a nice lady stops whilst I am crying,
I tell her I can't run anymore.

"Get in" she says, "I'll help you get back,
I'm a nurse" then she showed me ID.
I said I was scared that I'd let them all down,
But she said they'd be glad to see me.

We got to her house and she gave me a towel,
And then she rang the police from her phone,
She walked back in the room, and said "they're on their
way, your mum just wants you there back home."

A policeman came by, and picked me up,
I was scared that my mum would be mad.
"Don't worry" he said, "You just need your bed,
You're alright and everyone's glad."

"If you'd not been found within the next half an hour,
We were gonna put you on the TV."
And he then told me, last night they'd got a chopper,
Out all night looking for me.

NIGHTWALKING

A week or two goes by, we all seem closer for a while.
But then it wasn't too long before I'd felt the same way
again.

So one day, I'd decided to walk eight miles to Lichfield.
Nice walk actually. Past the canals and through a village
called Armitage, stopping along the way to wander around
some old stone house ruins.

Eventually I'd got there.
I wandered around and stayed in the park for an hour or
so, before walking to the town centre.
By now it was getting late.

Not sure if mum had sussed I'd ran off yet, so I made
sure that whenever I saw car headlights, to get out of
sight, behind a bin or a bush in someone's driveway.

I stayed in Lichfield for around two weeks, and managed
to get an hour of sleep at most each night, whilst
locking myself in the toilet cubical outside of the park.

If anyone knocked the door I'd just tell them it was being used, and more often than not usually just walk off in pursuit of a toilet elsewhere.

After nearly two weeks, and getting put off from trying to get sleep in the toilet cubicles, after one day finding some heavily soiled underwear dumped on to the floor. I was tired and hungry, and it was time to give myself up, and for me to go home.

I waved down a police car and told the officer that I'd ran away.
After telling him, he knew immediately who I was, and took me straight back home from there.

This time she hadn't seemed so happy to see me. I'd pissed her off big time, and I was indeed in the dog house.

I'd never plan to run off, but unknown to me then I think I'd started to get addicted to this sense of freedom that I'd been feeling.

Some sort of tranquil peace whilst roaming free, I guess.

The next time I'd ran away from home, was in the middle of the night, and once again I was trying to get myself to Stone.
Complete the mission or something I suppose.

I'd managed to hitch a lift a few miles down the road to Hixon, before being pulled up by a policeman, whilst walking the roads at three in the morning a few more miles away.

Again, mum wasn't happy at all.

Springfields estate, Rugeley

CROWN HOUSE

"Hurry up, Ben" my mum said to me, "We ain't got all
bloody day",
"We're off to Cannock, to see a psychologist, about all
your running away"

"Where are my glasses? And where are my fags? And
fucking hell where are my keys?"
"They're not under there Ben, I've already looked, just
get out the fuckin way please."

After five minutes, of stressing and panic, everything we
need has been found.
So we walk a few seconds, to the outside of Kwik Save,
and wait for the bus to come round.

It's not very often we go into Cannock - if anything it's
a day out.
I'm not really sure what we're going for, or really what
this is about.

I didn't know what to really expect, not that I'd thought
very much.
Because my life already had started to be, filled with
social workers and such.

I'd had no answers when people would ask, "Why is it
that you run away?"
But in front of your mum, who just doesn't agree, you
can't think of much you can say.

So we get to a building and walk up the stairs, and
we're asked to wait in a room.
A man with a smile says "We won't be a while, my
colleague is turning up soon."

He points to the cameras and says that they can hear
me, says there's no need to worry at all.
"It's to analyse, and there are two guys, behind the
mirror there on the wall."

"How do you feel, when you are at home?" the guy asked
me whilst sat in his chair.
But it's hard to express, let alone understand, and bring
it out with your mum there.

Every once in a while, I'll speak out my feelings, but it's
hard to see mum shake her head.
There's no point in me simply making things worse, so
it's better to say nothing instead.

They couldn't find answers, and no-one knew, why I just
couldn't stay home.
But there aren't any words, when you are so young, and
can't see that you just feel alone.

Tried to make me draw pictures, for some kind of hope,
that answers would come from my head.
But I want out of this joint, because I don't see the
point, I'd rather be elsewhere instead.

No use were the cameras, or men behind mirrors, to the
situation that we have here.
You'll never get answers, with kids feeling awkward, no
matter how small their fear.

When you really don't want to keep rocking the boat,
and adults will tell you you're wrong.
You don't know the places that are ahead, you're merely
just walking along.

TAMWORTH

One time too many,
Even with the doors locked I was escaping.
So many times now, that mum had said it.

It had always just sounded like a threat, but perhaps
now she needs the break.
I'm going into care.

"Go to school" she said, and soon enough before the end
of the day I'd met a social worker.
I'm going into a 'respite' foster home, which apparently
means I won't be there for very long.

Jean and Brian. Christian folk, they seemed welcoming
enough.
Two identical twin daughters, also friendly to me too.

We'd go to the local church every Sunday, but they knew
I preferred to be outside playing in the football pitch
cages.

No pressure, they can collect me after.

Mum would visit every now and then.
Felt special I guess.
Maybe things will get better.

Curing boredom by asking strangers for directions home,
in American accents.
Telling them that I was from Greenbow, Alabama.
Mis-correcting them, that it was a real place.

Six weeks had passed by, and we decided to give it
another try back home.
A fresh start.
New beginnings.
It all seems meaningful.
I hope so.

HAZEL AND GORDON

I knew that I was going back into care, because after a
few weeks things weren't working out.
"This is your warning, back in care by the morning, and
you're lucky you've not had a clout."

So the next day I had bunked off from school, and
thought I'd go to the social services myself.
It was better than having to be pulled into rooms,
looking at everyone else.

To my surprise when I walked around the corner, my mum
was already sat there.
And next to her, sat down was her fella, they'd come in
to put me in care.

Mum seemed surprised that I'd made my own way, and told
me that I'd had some cheek.
But I know that I'd rather be living elsewhere, I don't
want to stay one more week.

I went to reception and said to the lady, "I can't stay any
longer at home."
"Can I sit elsewhere? That's my mum on the chair, and
I just want to be on my own."

Not too long after, came a social worker, that found me
a room off the hall.
Then they asked me what I really wanted,
I said "I can't go back at all."

I walked out of the room, and then later that morning, a
social worker then said to me,
"We've struggled to find some long-term foster parents,
so we've found you some temporary."

"They live over in Chasetown, it's not far away, and it's
only for a week or two.
You'll have your own room, and we'll drive you there
soon, and your mum's packed a bag of clothes for you."

We then drove over to my first foster home, I met Hazel
for the first time when there.
Her husband, Gordon, he was at work, and her son, Jason
had popped out elsewhere.

She explained to me, that they were all quite chilled out,
and that I could help myself to the food.
But it took me a while before I'd even ask, just in the
case I was being rude.

Later on, I had met Gordon, like Hazel it seemed he was
cool.
The only time he got strict, with me at the house, was
with homework or trouble at school.

I didn't see much of their older son, Jason, but he'd
always been friendly to me.
It's the first time, in quite a while, that I'm where I feel
I can happily be.

Twice a week, Hazel and Gordon, would go to the working
men's club.
They'd take me with them, most of the time, and after
we'd all get some grub.

I'd always be playing at the pool table, Hazel and Gordon
would play dominoes.
Everyone in there always gave a warm welcome, I'm the
foster kid and everyone knows.

Out playing football, on the backfields, with the one or two new friends that I'd found.
Every few weeks I'd go out to play snooker, with a volunteer that would come round.

Gordon had always made me do my homework, when he'd got back from his day.
But not once did I think about stealing a thing, or think about running away.

Two months went by and I had forgot, that I would be moving one day.
Then they both said, "We do like you Ben, should we try and get you to stay?"

"That would be great" I said in reply, "I think you're both brilliant too",
"I can't promise a thing" Gordon then said, "But we'll call and see what we can do."

So I carried on, living my life, and actually going to school.
Still getting detention but starting to settle, everything in my life had felt cool.

I'm still no angel, but things could be worse, and nothing
I've done was too bad.
I'm feeling at home and unaware I'm content, and I don't
seem to drive no-one mad.

Then one day when I'd got back from school, Hazel asked
"Ben, can I please speak with you?"
"Social services rang, to say you're moving tomorrow,
we're sorry there's not much we can do."

"But this is long-term - you're moving to Rugeley, you'll
be living closer to all your family.
But I just want to say, you've done nothing at all, to
upset our Gordon or me."

"No worries" I said, I didn't want to cause trouble, and
kick up a big stinking fuss.
I'm used to it now, just moving around, and that was the
end of all us.

We all had a hug, and we said our goodbyes, and it felt
like a moment that meant.
And then the next morning, came the social worker, and
off to my new home I went.

RUNNING FURTHER
PART ONE

Once again I'm in a car, on my way to my new home.
Yet again I'm stepping in, to the land of the unknown.
And I know that I will be outside of their front door,
Knowing I'll be living there, not meeting them before.

But by now I guess that I, just take it as it comes.
It won't be bad, I guess I'm glad, I'm closer to my mum's.
My school is right around the corner, my family's house
ain't far,
And I guess I'm now intrigued, to find out who they are.

We walk up their garden path, the social worker knocks,
And I remember feeling, like a dog someone adopts.
I stand there with my bag, and then the front door
opens wide.
She's now my third foster mum, she says "Come on
inside."

I'm intrigued to meet the family, and everybody there.

I didn't know that I would be the only one in care.

At first it weren't a problem, but then over time,
I felt like the odd one out, like this home just weren't
mine.

Fighting with their older lad, and not much around to do.
Always kicked out from my school, suspensions through
and though.

So at night I'd pack a bag and walk to the edge of town.
Where I'd go, I would not know, and then flag a car down.

I once found myself in Birmingham, then walking to West
Brom.
Completely different sort of vibe, to the place that I've
come from.

I guess I just want something different, some sort of life
somewhere,
And I never think about food or sleep, when I'm walking
there.

Eventually try to get some rest, a bench there in the
park.

But it's hard to sleep when you see folk, walking in the dark.

Then after a week or so, I just can't go on anymore.
I say I'm sorry that I ran away, and they always ask "What for?"

The trouble is that by this point, I never really knew.
I had no answers for these things, on impulse that I'd do.

They'd caught me before a few times leaving, in the middle of the night.
My foster mum would make a drink and ask was I alright.

But I was soon to leave, this time in life had ended.
On one chilled out summer's day, when I had been suspended.

My foster mum was going out, and said "here's ninety pounds. Can you pay the bills man, when he comes?" and I said "sound."

"Only ten more minutes on that solitaire, and there is a rule. You can't be playing on computers, while you're off from school."

"Sure thing" I said, then said goodbye, and then she walked out of the door.
I carried on playing my game, and didn't think much more.

Then soon after I turned around to make myself a drink.
And on my way back, I saw the money, and then I had started to think. –

That's a load of money, I could escape, and get myself out of here.
I've never once seen a whole ninety pounds, it will probably last me a whole year.

If I take the time, to pack a bag, maybe someone will come back.
So I better hurry, with all of this money, and this time I'll leave my rucksack.

I look out of the window, to check that nobody sees me,
before darting out of the door.
I think this is the big one, and my heart is beating,
faster than it has done before.

RUNNING FURTHER
PART TWO

I dart out of the door and take a sharp left, and then
sprint through the nearby alleyway.
I know there's a train station across the road, and
plenty of time in the day.

Hope that nobody sees me and grasses me up, and I don't
know what time these trains come.
And only once have I ever even been on a train, when I
went to Walsall once with my mum.

I got to the station, in just a few seconds, and a train
had pulled in straight away.
I see there's a lady train guard standing there, so I
make my way over and say,

"Where does this train go?", and she then replied
"Birmingham", so I went onto the train.

Hope that I've not been spotted, and my heart is now racing, but at the same time I try to act plain.

The train then starts moving, and my hearts beating faster, a mix of excitement and fear.
I'm scared that the police might recognise me, and maybe they'll come onto here.

I've heard that Birmingham is a big place, and that is all I really know.
And no-one will think to look for me there, so that is where I will go.

I then get a ticket from the other train guard, hoping no questions are asked.
I pull out a twenty, because now I have plenty, and I'm leaving this place in the past.

"Child ticket?" he asks, and with "yes" I reply, and he gives me my ticket and change.
And I'm glad that the train's driving so far away, as it now starts to get out of range.

A few stations later, the train then stops at Bloxwich,
and on my carriage get on two police.
I hope they don't see me, because it's inside school
hours, but I'm wearing my tracksuit and fleece.

I'm crapping it now, will they recognise me? Am I about to
get caught by a cop?
But luckily, they both got off at Walsall, which
thankfully was the next stop.

Past Bescot Stadium and Tamebridge Parkway, past Villa
Park right into Brum.
I wonder by now if the police know that I'm missing, and
reported by my foster mum.

'Oh what a big tunnel, I've never done this', I thought
as the train pulled into New Street.
Tried my best to keep normal, and stay inconspicuous, as I
got up from my seat.

The doors opened, I got off the train, and then felt an
adrenaline stream.
First time in a city, whilst on my own tod, and the
furthest alone that I'd been.

I walked behind the commuters, they all seemed in a rush,
and then the main hall was where I got to.
Every time that I saw a police officer's clothes, I tried
my best to stay right out of view.

Convinced that they'd seen me, I'd quickly walk on, and
then turn my head over my shoulder.
Did not hang about, as I felt I stood out, because
everyone around was much older.

Walked outside of the station, and past some more police,
but I didn't spend that much time on the street.
I then turned around, to go back to the shop, to buy
myself something to eat.

And then I saw, the departure boards, and on the list I
then saw Coventry.
And I'd been fascinated by the designing of stadiums,
when I'd see the football on the TV.

So that's where I'll go, to Coventry's stadium, just have
a quick peek from outside.
So I find my way to the ticket office, and go on to pay
for my ride.

Back through the manned gates, and down to the train,
on the way to Coventry I now go.
It's been a good couple of hours since I had left, surely
by now they must know.

No police on this train, I'm now much more relaxed, as I
observe life around from this chair.
There are all sorts of people, going all sorts of places,
and it's not long until I get there.

I get off the train and then walk out of the station, to
try and find where Coventry play.
But there weren't many people, around to ask for
directions, and I had no clue of the way.

I walked back in to the station, didn't know what to do,
still hoping I'd not yet been seen.
And then I saw, in bright orange letters, "London
Euston" on the timetable screen.

'London Euston?' I thought, I wonder if that, is the
capital city or not.
And if it is, then that sounds exciting, I'd like to go
there a lot.

Or is it a village, in the middle of nowhere, that just happens to share the same name?
I don't want to be, stuck out in the sticks, like I was in Great Haywood again.

So I asked a man, waiting inside the station, "Excuse me mate could you help me?
Does that writing there, that says 'London Euston', mean 'London' as in the city?"

The man in his twenties then chuckled and said, "Yes mate that's the same place,
The train comes in five minutes, and arrives on this platform", in which I then replied to him "ace."

And when the train came, with excitement jumped on, the inside seemed well kept and plush.
As the train left, I once again, felt that same big intense rush.

The ticket inspector came up, I got out my cash, and said "A child single to London mate, please."
As I gave him my money, he then printed my ticket, and looked at me with slight unease.

"Where are you going, when you get to London?" the ticket inspector then suddenly said.
Then I had to think, of the quickest thing, which had come to me from inside my head.

"I'm meeting a pen-pal" I replied, "Where does he live?" the ticket man says.
"I can't quite remember", was what I'd thought to say, "but I'm staying there for a few days."

"Is anyone meeting you at the other end? Have you got a number for them you can call?"
In which I reply "his dad's meeting me there, and I don't have a number at all."

"So where are your bags?" he continues to ask, "Surely you have packed up some clothes?"
"His dad's lending me some", was the answer I thought, and I start to wonder if he now knows.

"OK" he then said and he gave me a ticket, and then walked off once I'd said "thank you".
A big sigh of relief, I can once again breathe, as I sit and I think to myself 'phew'.

But it's not over yet, could have he called the police?
Will there be some at the other end?
Or did he believe, my quick made up story that I was off
to see my friend?

The train pulls into Euston station, I can't believe
that I've made it here.
I get that same rush, that I've been getting all day, the
mix of excitement and fear.

Don't let the police see me, I try and act straight, in the
middle of the crowds I will stay.
But my chances of getting caught now feel a lot slimmer,
because I'm feeling so far away.

And then I walk into the main hall, still early and got
loads of time.
Make my way through the station, and then I see, a big
London underground sign.

I'd only once seen that red and blue symbol, on my mum's
computer game.
With some tunnels you'd walk through, with no tracks
at all, I didn't think that there'd be a train.

So for a few moments, in my mind I had thought, they
were just tunnels to walk underground.
Until I'd seen, all the ticket machines, and then down
below I heard a train sound.

I looked at the map, and I couldn't believe, the number of
stations I saw.
I know that I now, can get away, like I've not got to
before.

This time it's different, I've got money to travel, another
ticket I can afford.
I read names of some places that I'd vaguely heard of,
mainly from the Monopoly board.

Piccadilly Circus, Waterloo, King's Cross and Leicester
Square.
Leicester Square looks quite easy to get to from here,
so I think that I will go there.

I buy a ticket and get down to the train, everything feels
so busy to me.
Its hustle and bustle, and people look different, I feel
that there's so much to see.

I didn't realise that the stations were close, I was
surprised how quick I'd got there.
The train felt so fast, as it had passed, through the
tunnels and then to Leicester Square.

The train soon pulls in, and I leave the tube station, and
I take a short wander around.
The first time I'd seen buskers and human statues, and
homeless folk there on the ground.

Portrait artists and tourists with maps, all different
nationalities.
I heard Foreign-spoken languages all around me, and
there seemed to be lots of Chinese.

Not too long after whilst still walking around, it had
then started to lightly rain.
And I wasn't sure, if it would star to pour, so I went
back to get on the train.

I look at the map and I then see Piccadilly Circus is just
one stop away.
And I've never been, to once see a circus, so there for a
while I will stay.

Unknown to me then, it was only a few yards walk
through Coventry Street.
I'd brought one more ticket, got back on the train, but
had walked more than I'd sat in my seat.

I saw the bright lights that you'd see on the postcards,
it felt like I was at the fair.
See yet more buskers, and tourists would get henna
tattoos whilst sat on a chair.

I wandered around, and absorbed it all in, still with no
plan or no purpose.
I then asked a man in a group out on the town, "Excuse
me mate where is this circus?"

"This is it mate" he then replied, "There's no circus?"
I had then asked.
"It's not that kind of circus, it's because of the road",
he said as so many folk passed.

Not too long after, I made my way back, back on to the
underground.
And once again looked at the tube map, to see what
places could be found.

'Angel' sounded an interesting place, felt like something would be there.
But I soon got bored, with not much to do, so I decided that I'd go elsewhere.

I walked back to the tube, and then looked at the map, and saw 'Arsenal' next to a blue line.
I supported that team, and to go to Highbury, was a newfound childhood dream of mine.

After asking the staff inside the tube station, if that was where Arsenal play.
I then once again got on a train, sat down this time and made my way.

And to my surprise, the station was busy, plenty of folk were walking in.
And outside of the tube was a bloke selling scarfs, and flags from inside of a bin.

A game had been on, there at Highbury, so I made my way up to the ground.
The gates were still open and people were leaving, so I went inside to look around.

Up a few stairs and through the long hall, to the top
corner of the end stand.
I imagine they're playing, and Ian Wright's scoring, and
then in front of my face waves a hand.

"I'm sorry mate, but you've got to leave, we're emptying
the stadium now",
"No worries" I said, because I was just glad, that I'd
caught a good look somehow.

Out of the stadium, and back to the tube, I don't really
know where to go.
So I rode the tube back to Piccadilly Circus, where
buskers would put on a show.

The sound of loud bongos, and folk having fun, when I
got there it had now turned to night.
And it ain't gone dead quiet, like where I am from, and the
vibe at the time felt alright.

I walked down the street, where I saw a souvenir shop,
so I buy myself a wallet from there.
And then soon I see, that I have quickly, wandered back to
Leicester Square.

I walk past the buskers, and the Pizzerias, and the tube station that I now know.
But time's ticking on, and I still haven't found, any kind of shelter to go.

Back to the tube map, now where do I go, somewhere safe this time of night?
And then I saw, Whitechapel station, and thought that it sounded alright.

Surely I'm safe, near some big white chapel, it doesn't sound a busy place.
No-one will be around there at night surely, which means that few will see my face.

I buy yet one more ticket, still plenty of money, and I feel like a millionaire.
Through the barriers, and down the escalators, a Rasta busker plays Bob Marley there.

I change at Kings Cross, learn to read the tube map, get on the Hammersmith and City line.
I'm sure it will be quite a beautiful place, and this big white chapel will be fine.

THE BIG WHITE CHAPEL

The train pulls into Whitechapel, I've come from
Leicester Square.
The first thing that I notice, is the smell that's in the
air.

A unique musty dusty smell that I'd not found before.
It hits you as you're walking out of the underground
train door.

I look out for the exit signs, and then find my way out.
It's time to see, what this big white chapel is all about.
I walk onto the high street, see an empty market stall,
A twenty-four hour Seven-Eleven, and the Royal London
Hospital.

I take a left, walk down the road, and it's now late at
night.
I'm walking for a while now, and no chapel in sight.

I walk past the Blind Beggar pub, and to myself I said,
This clearly isn't the way to go, I'll turn back round
instead.

I walked up to the first person I saw, a British-Asian
man.
And said "Hi mate, I just wondered if you'd help me if you
can."

"What's up?" he said, then I replied "Mate, could you
tell me please is there, some kind of big white chapel
place, at all round here somewhere?"

"No" he replied, "not around here" he said with a warm
smirking smile.
"The nearest thing, we've got to that, is a mosque down
the road half a mile."

"Alright" I said, "thanks very much" I guess that I still
felt OK,
So I walked down the street, and just followed my feet,
and turned left down a dark alleyway.

Not sure where I'm going, or what I should do, is there
one of those hotel things about?
And whilst in the alleys, it was the first time, I'd ever
seen a down-and-out.

Wearing three coats, wild hair and a beard, and he spoke
to himself with a stare.
We had to cross paths, and he looks a bit mad, so I kept
on my guard and aware.

I looked in his eyes, and he looked in mine, and he simply
just walked straight passed me.
But the only time, I've seen a real tramp like that, is on
films in New York on TV.

Then a short-skirted and skimpy dressed lady, came up to
me and then said,
"Alright there love, do you want any business? Twenty
quid if you want head."

"I'm alright love, thanks" I then replied, "Alright
goodnight, sweetheart" she then said.
I think that it's time that I got out of here, I'll go back
to the station instead.

I see there's a turning just a few yards ahead, and I
think it leads back to the street.
Then I hear some shouts, from the bottom of there, so I
stop and try to be discreet.

I look down the alley to the other end, I see there are
three silhouettes.
Two standing up and one on the ground, I analyse all of
the threats.

"Try and grab me? You fackin bastard!" I hear as one
gives in the boot.
I think that I better stay out of the way, so I think to
myself I should scoot.

As I was just about to turn back around, one of the
voices then shouted to me,
"It's alright mate, this guy tried to rob us, you can walk
past this way we're friendly."

I don't remember saying too much, but I remember taking
a few steps ahead.
And said "alright thanks", and took my chance, "you're
not from around here" she then said.

"Nah" I replied. She asked "where you from? I can tell you're from up north somewhere."
"Birmingham" I then said, before she replied, "Have you ran off from home or from care?"

"Nah" I went on, "I've been kicked out from home", felt best that the truth was not told.
"How old are you mate?" she then asked me, and I said I was eighteen years old.

She then asked my name, and I did not want one person out there to find me.
So I thought of a name, as quickly as I could, and told her my name was Toby.

She said "hang with us, I can help you, get a place for you to stay for tonight.
My name is Joanne, and this girl is my friend", so I then replied "Thank you, alright."

The geezer she'd booted was still on the floor, a suited drunk Somali man.
We walked through the alley, to Whitechapel High Street, still really without a plan.

I asked her age, "thirteen" she replied, "I'm from here
but I've ran away,
From my foster parents, at my home in Kent, and I know
you have too" then she'd say.

"Alright Joanne" a lady interrupted, "I've scored but do
you have some ash?"
Then Joanne asked me, if I had cigarettes, or could I buy
some with my cash.

I pulled out a ten and gave it to her, her mate then
brought ten Lucky Strike.
"Why does she need ash?" I then said to Joanne, she
replied "it's to smoke a crack pipe."

Whilst outside waiting, Joanne had said, "You can't fool
me mate, I've seen.
That you don't know the streets, I can see you're naive,
there's no way on earth you're eighteen."

"You've ran away from foster parents or something, how
old are you really, come on?"
So I confessed the truth that I was just twelve, and
where I had really come from.

We then took a walk, through the streets of the East
End, through Aldgate then into Brick Lane.
We'd met Joanne's friends that were walking the roads,
and selling themselves on the game.

After a while, we'd made our way back onto Whitechapel
High Street.
Joanne then said, "I just got to do one more thing then
we'll go eat."

We walked down the road, and she's trying to find, one
of the girls that's around.
She meets her friend, on the game and on drugs, outside
of the underground.

"Come" then she said, "we've just got to do, something
it will just take an hour",
So I followed on, just tagging along, the freedom felt
like I had power.

And then we walked onto the back streets, a group of
drug addicts where there.
Joanne then said, "Can you lend me a score? I've seen
that you've got money there."

"What's a score?" I then asked, and then she replied,
"Twenty quid, I'll give it you back by tonight."
Seriously Toby, I swear you can trust me",
so I said, "OK, alright."

"I'll just be a minute, I swear I'll come back, just stay
here and don't go nowhere".
She said as she walked, down the alleyway, and I felt a
bit lost standing there.

Out of the blue, two guys come to me, one with a
Mohawk hair-cut and green vest.
A thick Irish accent, said "give us your money, or I'll
stick this thing into your chest."

I looked down below, saw it was a flick-knife, he then
puts the blade up to my face.
"Just give us that wallet, we've seen you've got money,
or I'll cut ya all over the place."

"Alright" I said, "I'll give you the wallet, but get that
thing away from me",
So I handed over, my newly brought wallet, which had in
it all the money.

Just a few seconds later, Joanne came back, and I think
she could tell I felt bad.
"You aright babes?" she said and so I replied, "No those
men just took all that I had."

"He pulled out a knife, and they took my wallet, and now
what am I gonna do?"
"Who took it?" she asked, I looked round then I said,
"Those guys in the green and the blue."

"Oi you! You cunts", she shouted over, as she walked up
to them fast with rage.
"Give me back his wallet, or I swear I'll punch ya", I was
surprised at her brass for her age.

"Please don't hit me, I'm sorry Joanne", the Irishman
pleaded out loud,
Before falling down, and then crying out,
"Please don't hit me, when I'm on the ground."

Joanne took the wallet, and said "He's on the street,
you don't go and rob off your own",
"I'm sorry Joanne" he then said crying out, "I wasn't
sure when I saw him alone."

"It don't fackin matter, if he was alone, you don't rob
from those on the streets,
Don't ever let me see you do that again, or you're dead
you fackin tealeaves."

"I'm not robbing you Tobes, but I'll keep hold of this
wallet, you don't know these streets like I do.
There are all kinds of people, in this place around here,
and loads will try to rob you."

So I agreed, and I gave her my trust, and we both walked
off again.
Tagging along, and I followed Joanne, then we got back
to Brick Lane.
I'd meet more of her friends on corners of roads, some
would look at me and then they'd say,

"Who's this guy Joanne?" and she would reply, "He's
from 'Bermanam' and he's ran away."
We later arrived, at a busy flat, me and Joanne had sat
on the floor.
First time in my life that I'd see people, looking this
rough before.

Some asking for ash, or searching for foil, and making a pipe from a can.
I just observed, and sat there content, as their drug session began.

"You want some of this Jo?" said a voice from the bathroom, "Of course I do" then Jo replied.
Then I stumbled in, to her smoking a pipe, even though she'd tried to hide.

"Don't you ever smoke this", she then said to me, "I'll slap you if I see you smoke crack.
I know you see me now, but trust me its evil, and really I just want my life back."

"Go back in the room, I'll be back in a minute", she said and so I made my way.
I sat back on the floor, and smoked a fag once more, it's getting light, soon will be day.

They seemed friendly enough, although one guy, would talk to himself whilst sat still.
"Don't worry about him", Joanne said to me, "he's harmless but mentally ill"

The man near me, lifted up his crack can, and said
"Joanne do you want a lick?"
"Of course" she replied, and then squatted down, and
sucked on the crack-can quite quick.

"What about your mate? Is he having some?" he asked
her and then she said to him,
"Not in a million years, don't you dare give him crack, if I
see you I'll kick your head in."

Not too long after in came the police, with a warrant for
someone's arrest.
The police said it was for suspicion of murder, for
stabbing someone in the chest.

"Whose is that kid?" one copper then said, as he saw
me sat down on my own.
Joanne then replied, "he is my cousin", then the copper
said "get him back home."

Jo and I left, and as we walked down the road, she'd
warned a friend the police were there.
Then she said to me, "I think you should go back, it's
not safe here you're better in care."

"I'm not going back" I say in reply, the thought of it
had made me stressed.
She said "Alright then, I'll take you under my wing, I
know somewhere that we can get rest."

It was now early morning, and we walked to Poplar, she
told me about her friend on the way.
"I've been a good mate and he owes me a favour, he's
also schizophrenic and gay."

"Schizophrenic?" I ask and say "What does that
mean?", she replied "Fruity loops, lost the plot.
He often thinks, that people have a gun, and goes mad
when he thinks he'll be shot."

"Don't worry" she said, "you'll be fine with me, he
trusts me unlike he does most",
When we got to his flat, she said, "Wait over there," so
I stood outside by the lamppost.

Five minutes went by, and it looked like he was out, she
said "I know him, and I know that he's in",
So once again, she shouts out his name, and then she
tells me that he is coming.

He opens the door, slightly ajar, before closing it to
unlock the chain.
I was her cousin, who'd run off from up north, she would
then to him explain.

He let us in, and went straight back to bed, after giving
Joanne a blanket.
Joanne had a wash, then made us some squash, then we
sat in the room and drank it.

"Do you think that we should, try and block the door, in
the case he goes mad and kicks off?"
Joanne had asked me, and so then I would agree,
"Yeah look at that table he's got."

So we both got up, and moved his table, so that he
couldn't open the door.
Then Joanne lay down, and threw me some cushions, from
the sofa to put on the floor.

She had soon seen that I'd not got a blanket, and
offered me the one that she'd got.
I politely refused "Nah I'll be alright, you have it but
thanks a lot."

"Come share this with me, then we'll both be warm, you can bring those cushions" she said.
It's been a long night, my first in this city, and I'm glad to be resting my head.

THE DELLOW

"Let's get some food" said Joanne, "We'll jump on the
tube train,
Walk straight up from Whitechapel, to a soup-kitchen
off Brick Lane."

"What is a soup kitchen?" I had then replied,
"They give you food" Joanne then said, "and let you go
inside."
And then soon we got there to see a lady at a door,
She asked our names and said to Jo that she'd seen
her before.

"He's my cousin" Joanne said, the lady asked my name
and age,
"Toby Sycamore and I'm seventeen", she then wrote on a
page,
On the clipboard she was holding, "What's your date of
birth please mate?"
I replied the "fifteenth of October, nineteen seventy-
eight."

She let me in but when she'd sussed, I was called over
to be seen,
"The date of birth you gave me means that you're
nineteen."

I'm not sure how I blagged it, but I fibbed my way out,
And went and joined Joanne, when I heard her shout.
I glanced across the busy room, the first time I had saw,
So many different types of people, in one room before.

Junkies, crack heads, down-and-outs, some that were
insane,
OAP's, refugees, and prozzies from Brick Lane.

Cockneys, Irish, English, Scottish, the odd one from
Pakistan,
It's nearly time that I get served, before me just one
man.

"Bless you sister, ever so kind", he said as she passed
him a bun,
And that's when I had realised; the lady serving was a
nun.

She offered him a piece of cake, and then passed him a
bowl,
In which the cockney bloke replied, "Thank God, bless
your soul."

And then it came to my turn, I smiled and said, "Hello",
I asked how much the food would cost, I really didn't
know.

"It's free" she said, "Have what you like", in a southern
Irish voice,
So I looked on through the glass, feeling somewhat
spoiled for choice.

"I'll have some of that paste-bake, please if that's
OK?"
"Sure it is" she then replied, as I held up my tray.

A piece of cake I was also given, I said my thanks and
turned around,
Joanne asked me to find a seat, and said later she'd sit
down.

I looked across the busy room, to try and find somewhere
to eat.
And near the middle, saw a gap, with an empty seat.

I made my way through the gap, of all the eating folk,
To the seat I saw was spare, and then I asked the old
bloke.

"Is it alright to sit here? I don't want to intrude",
"It's OK kid", the old man replied,
"Just enjoy your food."

I started to eat my pasta-bake, and then I heard a shout,
A bloke in his fifties looked in my direction, I hadn't a
clue what it all was about.

I turned my head to see behind, but nothing had gone on.
"Yeah, you" the bloke then further shouted, "Where
have you come from?"

"From Birmingham" I then replied, confused why he would
shout,
He asked my age so I said, seventeen and been kicked out.

"Seventeen my arse" he said with a growl, "piss off kid
go on,
You shouldn't even be in here, go back to where you're
from."

Then from across the room I heard, a chair slamming
loud and quick,
A guy in his twenties then stood up, and shouted "Oi you
fackin prick",

"Leave that fackin kid alone, pick on someone your own
size."
"It's alright mate, your welcome here", he said whilst
looking down into my eyes.

The man who had told me to go, then frowned and shook
his head,
"He shouldn't even be in here, he should be home
instead."

"You can't fool me, no way kid, are you seventeen you
no",
"Just leave him alone" the other bloke said, "He's
probably got nowhere to go."

And soon there came a peace again, we all just ate our food,
The younger guy then came back and said "sorry that he's rude."

"If he starts on you again, just come straight to see me,
If he thinks that he can push you around, then trust me he'll soon see."

I left the Dellow with Joanne, but from now I guess this place,
Is somewhere that I'll often come and be my saving grace.

And over time it's now a place that I know I can,
Ask someone if I need to find again Joanne.

The Dellow centre, Aldgate.

EAST END ADVENTURES

I walk the streets of East London, with my newfound
friend.
From Bethnal Green to Limehouse, Aldgate to Mile End.
From Bow Road to the Isle of Dogs, Shadwell to
Stepney Green,
I know that still, back at home, they've no clue where
I've been.

All my money had ran out, and gone by the fourth day,
Even though, I'd got back that twenty, Joanne promised
to pay.
At first we would be staying, at one of Joanne's pals.
But often be back at Brick Lane, meeting the street
gals.

We'd often be in Whitechapel, and Joanne would always
say,
"I'll meet you back here in two hours, just hang around
and stay."

So I'd hang by the tube station, with the drunks on the street.
And Ozzie he was African, had no shoes on his feet.

Couldn't understand a word he said, he chewed on Khat all day.
I'd kick an empty metal can, and they'd join in and play.

Sometimes people would walk past, and give a little smile,
They hadn't seen something like this, on this street for a while.

We'd sometimes visit Joanne's friend, in the hospital ward.
I think he liked us both being there, it helped him stop being bored.

His name was Drew, a Scottish man that had been beat up bad.
And all his leg was in a cast, but Drew never seemed sad.

I'd tell folk outside the tube station, that I needed to get home.
Asked for money for a ticket, or to use the phone.

I'd often make around a tenner, or sometimes I'd make
more,
And now I've hustled up more money, than I ever made
before.

An old drinker had been watching me, sat on a crate down
on the ground.
He winked at me when he had seen, that I'd hustled up
five pound.

"Nice drop, kid" he said "You did that good, could I please
ask you summut?
I promise you kid that I will pay you back, could you please
just lend me a nugget?"

"What's a nugget?" I reply, "A quid, a pound" he then
said.
"I just need a tin to settle my nerves, and help me get
back a straight head."

"I promise you lad, I'm a good man, and I keep to my word
all the time",
So I then gave him, a one-pound coin, and said "Alright
mate, that's fine."

"Come over here, I'll show you some things" said the old
Irish drinker to me.
"I'll soon give you back, that pound that I'd lent, sit on
this crate and you'll see.

Don't say a word when I speak to the people, but if they
give us some money say thanks.
Because if you're polite, even if you feel shite, they could
come back and there's always a chance."

"Even if they ignore you, you've got to stay strong, just
say to them have a nice day,
Don't be like those that just cuss and swear, you can't
let your feelings get in the way."

So we sat on the crate and some people approached,
"How are you, sir?" the drinker then asked.
The guy on the street replied "Alright, I'm sweet, how
are you?" as he walked passed.

"It could always be worse" the old drinker replied, "You
don't have any spare change please do you?"
And then the man went to give him a pound, then
changed his mind and gave us two.

"Oh thank you so much, that's so kind of you sir, I hope
that you have a nice day",
And then he would tell me, to make a point, of thanking
them as they walked away.

"Always be nice", he said to me, "and you'll get regulars
come all of the time.
And here's that nugget that I promised you back, see I
stuck to those words of mine."

"Thanks mate" I replied.
Later I'd met Joanne as she had walked by.
I did not know myself that I had just learned, a new trick
that I was to later try.

I'd been missing a month by this point until now, and
Joanne said that I had to phone home.
To let them know that I'm safe so we went to the
station, and walked inside to use the phone.

She pressed one-four-one to withhold the number, and
then I dialled it in on the keys.
Then I passed the phone, straight to Joanne, and said
"Can you do it please?"

They asked where I was but I wouldn't say, if I did I thought I'd be a fool.
So instead of them looking in London for me, I said I was in Liverpool.

Whitechapel Road

TAKEN BACK

I've been away a while now, and it sort of feels,
I've forgot that I'm a runaway - I guess I'm feeling free.

No point in calling them back home, they'll know I'll be
alright,
Well that's what I think anyway, that no-one is missing
me.

Here I have a life, can go on my own way.
I'm not stressing anyone out and I'm loving every day.
Ain't got into no trouble here, ain't got into no strife,
In my mind I see my family, just getting on with life.

I'm glad for them. I'm glad that they don't have to put
up with me.
They won't find me here, I'll stay forever, London is
where I'll be.

Someday soon I'll get a job, and then rent my own place,
But for now, just make sure that Old Bill don't see my
face.

I'd got to meet some of Joanne's family, in a Poplar flat.
A big London-Irish East End lot, who later told me that,
I should go home because people will be worried about me.
"Nah they won't" I would reply, guess then I didn't see.

The real dangers of this world, what goes through
people's minds.
I never thought that folk would wonder, was I still alive?
As long as I'm not in the way, no problems that I'll
cause.
And ride it out till I'm sixteen, free from all the laws.

Joanne's family said we should go to the police, and tell
them that I've ran away.
So there'd been a plan that her uncle and me, go to the
police station that day.

We walked for a bit then we saw the police station, and
then Jo's uncle pointed and said,

"Good luck then kid, I'll leave you here, don't come back,
stay up north instead."

I walked into the police station, felt like my dream was
ending.
Back into the old world, and now there's no pretending.
Like being awoken from a dream with acceptance, friends
and adventure.
Back to people writing notes about my life on paper.

I walked up to the station desk, and said that I'd ran
from,
My foster parents in the midlands, and two months I'd
been gone.
They said to me "Alright please wait, for someone to see
you there",
So I hung around, and then sat down, on the police
station waiting room chair.

A minute went by, and my heart was beating, I didn't want
this trip to end.
So I said to the police, I was going out for a smoke, but
it was all just pretend.

I looked around, there was no sign of Jo's uncle, so I
just ran straight out of the place.
All the way down the road, with a few left and rights,
and hoped the police weren't giving chase.

Got back to Whitechapel, and that night found Joanne,
who said she'd guessed that I'd ran away.
And we stayed at her mates, so the police couldn't find
me, and then I roamed around town the next day.

It's all back to normal, I'm still here and I'm hustling,
And asking for change for the phone,
Or blagging a story that I'm stranded in Whitechapel,
and I need a travelcard to get home.

And then a week or so later, I'm in the hospital, visiting
Drew, and I'm sat by his bed.
Then bursts in Jo's sister, who shouted over "Where's
Jo? Move and you're dead!"

"Call the security!" she shouted out loud, "that lad
there - he's ran away",
She grabbed me by the scruff of the neck and said, "Kid
you're going home today."

Two security guards ran upstairs, there's no escape
from here.

This hospital is too big for a chase; I doubt that I will
get away.
OK. Hands up, I'm a runaway.

"You're not going anywhere until the police get here"
said Joanne's sister,
It had now sunk in, that this was the end of my
adventure unfolding.

Later she calmed and had explained to me, that she had
deeply been worried for Jo.
"You both should be at home, not out on the streets,
she's got in all kinds of trouble you know."

The police then soon arrive, and take me down into a van,
And just before I go through the door, I catch a glimpse
of Joanne.
The police take me back to the station, where I see her
again too,
And then I'm put into the cells, until the police know
what to do.

But I don't want to go back to my foster parents. I guess that I'm feeling ashamed,
Of what I've put them through, think I need somewhere new, guess I'm afraid to take my own blame.

And feeling the one that causes the trouble, feeling the one that causes the stress,
If I could only start all this again, it wouldn't all seem such a mess.

I'm picked up from the police station by people they called 'escorts',
That there's a reason for.

Because if you need the toilet at some point on the way,
They'll hold your arm and walk with you, right up to the door.

This toilet here has got a window, but I'm too tired - the game is up.

Time to embrace something new, what will my life bring.
One night in a kid's home, downstairs on the sofa, and then when morning came, driven to the social services offices.

Hours going by, waiting around.
So boring.

Nowhere for me to go, the numbers of foster parents
are too low, eventually they found some respite ones in
Penkridge.

Nice folk they were, two weeks or so I was meant to be
there, living in Penkridge in their care.

But Penkridge was a quiet place.
Me? Coming straight from the east end?
Kicking a football around in an empty field can only do so
much for a restless soul like me.

And before I knew it, I'd gone out for a walk, or so I said.
But this time knew in my head, where I was going, and
what I was doing.
If I could do it before, then I can do it again.
London isn't so far, not far at all.

I know that I can get there.
I'll hitchhike or hide inside train toilets - a small risk
worth taking.

At some point I'm booted off the intercity train, and then
I'm on the motorways.

Cars and lorry drivers, drop me place to place,
Before I know it, conversations have helped pass the
time.
"Thank you mate, yes this tube station will do me just
fine."

And so I make my way, back to the east end.
If I hang round long enough, I know I'll find my friend.
If the prostitutes have seen her, I know that they'll tell
me,
They passed on the message, and then that evening, I
had seen Joanne.

For some reason, things seemed normal again.

Don't ask me why, I'll never know, maybe one day I might.
But for now I'm not quite sure, but this is the path
that I'm now on.

TOBY SYCAMORE

Again I'm in London, and I'm back on the run,
And because I was grassed up before,
I need to stay undetected, so that nobody finds me,
I'm going to have to try more.

No-one can know that my real is Ben, and that I've ran
away from care,
Folk will be asking for me around Whitechapel, so it's
best they think I've not been there.

So I speak a fake accent, a pretend East End cockney,
from the moment I wake up, until night.
For the whole next four months, with everyone that I
meet, just so I know that I'm alright.

Or else they might find me, when Old Bill ask questions,
someone might say, "I know him".
So if everyone thinks that I'm from round here,
The chances I'm caught are quite slim.

One day plain-clothes police pulled me outside Victoria
station, asking people outside for spare change.
They were gonna release me, but decided they couldn't, as
I was young and my story seemed strange.

The address that I gave, just didn't exist, which I'd said
in my fake cockney voice.
And two-and-half hours later, they still wouldn't release
me, I knew I did not have a choice.

"Hands up I've been caught, I'm not really from here",
I said like I spoke when back home.
I thought they'd go mad, but in the end I was glad, that
it all ended in humourful tone.

"You did have us fooled, we thought you were local,
it was just the address that you gave,
Which had made us suspicious, or else we would have
released you out onto your way."

Well its more lessons learnt for the next time I guess,
as I wait to be brought home by escort.
If you need to stop for the bog, they'll walk you right to
the door, but the lift home there's time for some
thought.

A few hours later I'm well on my way, and I know at
least I'll get a warm bed.
Once I get back to the kids home where I live,
I'll wash all my clothes and get fed.

But everyone knows that I'll soon be back, via
hitchhiking or bunking the train.
And I'll always choose a different way to get there, it
may be unwise to pick the same.

From Winnersh Triangle, Watford Gap, Oxford, Milton
Keynes,
I'm searching for my independence.
Nothing stops these dreams.

I know that I can make my way, back to find Joanne.
Just go the way they least expect, was usually my plan.
Often I would walk through town, through Pinner, St
Johns Wood.
As long as no-one knows I'm Ben, I'll reckon I'll be good.

ABBEY ROAD

Joanne has gone for the day, and by now I know what for,
And today I've found a travelcard, lying on the floor.
I think today that I'll explore, some more of London town,
I know that it won't be for hours that Joanne will be around.

So I head into the station, stare at the map whilst still,
And from there I then decide, that I'll go to Grange Hill.
There must be surely something there, cool for me to see,
Or they wouldn't make a kids programme, about it on TV.

So I take the tube into town, change on the central line.
And on the way I ask a lad, that's near me for the time.
We end up talking, I explain, that I'm off to see somewhere.
But it seemed from what he'd said, that there was nothing there.

So I looked at the tube map, to find a place again,
And thought I'd travel to Swiss Cottage, just because
the name.
Eventually I got there, and then soon I saw,
A pub that was the old Swiss Cottage, but there was
not much more.

And so I see a close by station, is called St Johns Wood,
That sounds like it could be pleasant,
I'll go - it could be good.
And so I head there on the tube, and walk in wander-
mode,
And before I know it, I find myself in Abbey Road.

"Abbey Road? As in the Beatles?" I didn't really know,
And then I see some people there, posing for a photo.
On the zebra crossing, walking behind one another,
Trying their best the replicate, the Beatles album cover.

I read the writing on the wall of the studio,
Before I'd felt I'd seen it all and was time for me to go.
Not sure what I can do now, to stop myself being bored,
And so I read the free magazine that I'd picked up before.

Towards the back I saw a number, a chat-line free to
call,
I thought that I would check it out and have a laugh,
that's all.

But it turned out, that for only women was it free,
But still I pressed the button that they would press,
just to see.
"Leave a message", said a voice, and completely for a
joke,
I pretended I was a London girl, looking for a bloke.

Just bored, I guess, and wasting time, entertainment's
what I need,
But I really would not have ever guessed, where this all
would lead.
I later dialled the number again, and laughed quite hard,
for quite a bit,
That some local London lad, had gone and fell for it.

He said she sounded interesting, but oh, when will I learn,
I should have stopped it all right then, but the message
I'd return.

Pretend East-End cockney girl, surely he will suss,
But he's quickly messaged back, saying he wants to meet
us.
Surely Ben you're not so cruel, to keep this wind-up
going?
But it spiralled out of control, before I was knowing.

The guy had asked 'her' for a meet, so I messaged him
back "Okay",
He still hadn't sussed out, and we'd agreed, to meet up
later that day.

I couldn't resist not knowing at all, whether my little
cheeky plan worked,
So I went to the tube, where we said we would meet, sat
down on the floor and observed.
At first there wasn't anyone there, but then I had
clocked,
A twenty-something year old, kept looking round had
stopped.

"That must be him" to myself I thought, as I watched
and could see,
He was clearly standing outside there, waiting for
somebody.

I thought "you mug", inside I laughed, before I had felt
bad,
I kinda feel sorry now, he must be feeling mad.

Without thinking I walked up and said "Hi, we don't know
one another,
But you were speaking to my sister, and I'm her younger
brother."

"She's been delayed and has had some problems" I then
further say,
"She told me to come and tell you, that she's half an
hour away".

"What's up?" he asked, "is she ok?" I had to think of
something quick,
"She's having trouble with her ex-fella, and he's a bit
of a dick."

Now really I don't have a clue, of why I had then said,
"She said it would be easier, to meet in Bow instead"
So we then had got on a bus, and after ten minutes or
so,

I jumped up and sprinted off, whilst saying "sorry got to go."

I got off the bus and then ran down the road, the guy I was with looked confused.
I know my joke has now gone way too far, at first I had been amused.

I've had my fun, now for today, and done all of my exploration,
I know that my walk won't be too far, back to Whitechapel station.

CHANGING

Things aren't like they were before, I don't see Joanne
that much.
But always by the end of night, the start of day, she'll
help me find somewhere to sleep, after we have gone to
eat.

It's six in the morning, pigeons are walking along the
pavement and into the road, only just beating the litter-
truck with orange flashing lights, that has come to
sweep the streets.

The cobbled roads just off Brick lane are almost empty,
only the last two prostitutes are now standing there.
But still a punter drives slowly down the road, a small
Bangladeshi man winds down his window to stare out.

I look from the bottom of the road, the street-gal talks
for a second before getting in.

Joanne's with the other girl, and they both walk the other way, she tells me to meet her later, so off I go, on my own.

She's always around Brick Lane these days, sometimes I worry about what she gets herself into, or what gets into her.

The little romance we'd had for a short while was now long gone.
How could I compete with grown-up men?

But still I'd hang around, and Joanne never abandoned me. I was always her pretend 'cousin' needing somewhere to stay.

Whitechapel too over time is now changing, and people don't hang around here so much anymore.

So my time is spent exploring, going to visit more tube stations that I've never been to, to see what is there, why such interesting names?

This time I'd gone to Seven Sisters, sounds quite welcoming, feminine and warm.
Not really sure where I was going, or what I was looking for, but by now it was getting late.

I sat on some railings asking passers-by for spare cigarettes, and then a lad approaches me, must be about eighteen.

He'd asked me for a cigarette, which I'd explained that mine were all blagged, but saved him half, easy come easy go and all that.

A local London lad, of African descent, seemed friendly enough when we had got talking.

Out of nowhere he grabs me, pointing something into my torso from inside his coat. In hindsight, it was probably nothing.
But back then I didn't know.

"Say a word and I'll shank you" he said, in which I replied "I've got nothing to fucking rob."

A lady in her mid-twenties had been walking towards us from inside the station.

"Now you're going to grab her bag" he said "and then you're going to make a run, but if you try and leg it from me, then I'll take you somewhere and I'll cut you up."

"Fuck off mate, I ain't doing that" I impulsively replied.
"You getting lippy?" was his response, accompanied with some sort of forced dark twisted stare.

"Do it now I mean it, or I'll shank you!" he said, still with his freakily forced tension.
But not even he could make me sink *that* low.

Looking back, maybe he'd had some weird plan, grab and pretend to catch me, act the good guy, and collect the reward.

I tried to run, but just couldn't out-do him.
Too fast, and too strong.
I'd pissed him off with my escape attempt, maybe I'd questioned his control.
So he pulled me towards him, once again reminding me of what could be my fate.

"You're coming with me" he said, so close that I could feel his breath after each and every word.

"Help!" I shout to the handful of people passing by. "Ignore him", interrupted my capture, "He's my brother and I'm taking him home."

The fact that he was dark black, and I was pale white didn't seem to make the slightest difference.
No-one seemed bothered.

Just another altercation in the street, nothing to stick their noses into.
Just confused gestures before looking away.

After leading me onto a bus, we got on through the back doors whilst the driver at the front had been distracted.
I'm made to walk upstairs before him.

"What's your problem anyway mate? What you doing this for? You're a fucking bully, picking on kids my age?"
So then he gets up, right to my face whilst towering above me. "Oh you think you're a big man now do you?"

I get ready to absorb a punch if one comes my way.
"Pussy ole" he cussed, before turning around, and as
he's gone to sit down, I've made a run.

Past the seats and onto the stairs, down to the doors
hoping they would open.
"Please let me off" I shout to the driver, "That lad's
threatened me with a knife, please let me off I'm worried
for my life."

Such a frustrating few seconds, the bus isn't moving
and the doors aren't opening, and I'm not sure what is
happening.
I plead again, and finally the doors open. But it's too
late, my new worst enemy drags me off the bus and leads
me down the road.

"I warned you" he said, "Are you asking to be killed? Pull
anything else like that and you're dead."

We soon get back to the tube station, through the
barriers and down onto the platforms, still holding my
jacket and breathing down my neck.

To the side of one of the platforms was a confectionary shop, he pointed to it and reeled off a shopping list of items that he wanted me to rob.

"If you don't do it, or you do another runner, I'm gonna really fuck you up" he quietly growled.

"Okay" I replied feeling somewhat confused.
Perhaps this was my chance, somewhere safe, to turn the tables.

He stood outside whilst I walked past the shop counter. "Please call the police mate, that lad has been holding me up with a knife", I say to the shopkeeper, at a low enough volume that the lad outside wouldn't have been able to hear me.

It's an intense moment as I hope for a reply. "Please just call the police", I plead yet again.
But nothing.

Just a confused gaze, like I'd been speaking in an alien language that he couldn't understand.

The lad outside had clocked me, and came waltzing into the shop.

"What are you doing?" he shouted, before dragging me out by my arm.

I've had more than enough for my liking now, so I decide to try and escape.

Perhaps my adrenaline could help me out-do him?
Now I feel confident, so I sprint along the platform and follow the exit signs.

He chases me whilst shouting out that I've tried to steal someone's handbag, and for people to grab me.
"He's lying" I shout, whilst trying to avoid barging the people that I'm running past.

I turn into another tunnel and run.
Ahead of me are two uniformed police in bright yellow jackets.
Thank fuck. I'm safe.

I tell them straight away that the guy has been leading me around with a knife.
And by then he came running up, pretending to be the Good Samaritan.

"OK look, I'm a runaway from the midlands" I said to the police, "But I ain't nicked no-ones bag."

Both police officers seemed somewhat confused with the situation at hand, and so led us both to separate rooms.
I'd made sure they got him away, and told them the whole story.

I knew that they wouldn't do me for some bodged up allegation of a robbery.
No proof, just lies, I know I'll be alright.

But yeah, I'm a runaway; hands up you've got me.
Time to go back, not sure where not to,
But guess that's now what I'm used to.

Back to a police station, inside a cell, waiting for hours for another escort.
But no hard feelings, the police are just doing their jobs.
No-one is being nasty, and they all seem sort of understanding.

Fourteen hours later, the cell door opens, a social services escort has come to take me back. Apparently word has it, that I'll be going in to a kid's home upon my return.

OLD PENKRIDGE ROAD

"There are no foster parents for you to go to today,
Only space in the kid's home in Cannock" they say.
"Might sound a bit daunting, but they ain't so bad,
And you might find that in the end that you're glad."

All different things the kids in there have been through.
Some have had some bad pasts, and some are like you.
They can be pleasant, it's not like its jail,
Although sometimes there are some kids there on bail.

You will get your own room, and you'll still go to school.
The staff in there are friendly, and there ain't no strict
rules.
They don't put kids in there, because they've done
something wrong,
And for you it's until, a new home comes along."

So I said "Alright then", and then tied up my lace.

Then we drove up to the kid's home, which did seem a
big place.
I looked into a window, and I thought this place was cool,
When I saw some other kids, in a room playing pool.

I soon met all the kids there, we'd joke and we'd laugh.
They gave me a warm welcome, and so did the staff.
Then one said "we're chillin, a load of us are upstairs,
You're welcome to come and hang out with us up there."

So then I went up, to where the kids where at,
They all welcomed me, and then inside I sat.
"You ever sniffed gas?" one lad there had then asked,
Before showing me how, as the deodorant was passed.

"Right through this jumper, the fumes in you breathe,
You'll get a mad buzz, like you won't believe."
So I pressed down the button, and through the rag I
breathed in,
I'm now seeing mad lines, and sounds I'm hearin.

Was that a voice? I really can't quite make out,
Faster, faster and faster, what's this all about?
It just wouldn't slow down and the faster it got,
Made me truly believe that my brain would soon pop.

I said "Whoa that's mental",
The rag and can I then passed,
It was my first time, but was not my last.

The deodorant ran empty and the buzz had soon slowed,
And that was my first day, at Old Penkridge Road.
For our lunch and for our tea, in would come a cook.
We'd choose from a small menu, which sort of felt like
luck.

And then when came Saturday, once we'd cleaned our
room and changed our sheets,
We'd all collect our pocket money, and then we'd hit the
streets.
I'd get just enough for ten fags, if I sold one or two,
To make enough so we could share, that's what we'd
always do.

Wasn't long before we were often, running out at night,
Breaking windows, smashing doors, some of us would
fight.
Walking round the children's home, needing to find the
staff,
To get permission to sign out, but don't know where
they're at.

I'd knock on the office door, signing out sometimes took
ages,
Because the staff were often in a meeting, or dealing
with someone's rages.
I remembered my mum telling me, my real father's name.
And so I tried to find him, time and time again.

I rang up all the local Westwood's, from inside the phone
book,
But couldn't find who I was looking for and had no luck.

A friend from school said I could sleepover, but then came
'what the heck?'
When they said that my mates parents, had to go
through a police check.

They said it would take six weeks,
but my mate said this weekend.
Fuck this shit I want my life,
I'm going back to the East End.

EDMONTON GREEN

I see the train approach, around the bend, from down the
bottom end.
Turn my head, hoping that no-one's seen me, they all
know by now, that I'm probably on my way to London.

The guard steps off the train.
I look down along the platform and nod at him, before
getting on and sitting down.

Once again my heart is quickly beating, whilst waiting for
the train doors to close.
What if they've been tipped off? And what if someone
knows?

Soon the guard walks along the train carriage, "Tickets
please", but this time I don't have one.
"My dad's not well and I need to get to him", another
blag reeled off in the moment.

Will I be in trouble? Will he call the police on me?

But luckily, he'd believed my story and in the end he'd let me stay.
I'm on my way once again, to Birmingham New Street.

But this time instead of wandering, there's no time to waste, by now they could be looking for me.
They've probably guessed where I will be, and I know that train to Coventry, will head straight into London town.

There's probably police on the lookout, I can't hang about, down the escalator, and onto the platforms I go.

The train is busy, which for me is good, it will take the guard a little longer,
To walk up the train.

Maybe so busy that he doesn't come at all, I hope so, because this time I've no money to pay.

Mums with prams, business folk with laptops, everyone's talking, to each other or on their phones.
I'm observing, peeking down the aisle, getting ready to dart into the toilet when I'd seen the ticket man.

A lot of people had got off at Coventry, and after that stop the train had seemed empty.

I did see the conductor, just once or twice, but wasn't too sure if he was checking for tickets, or just walking along the train.

After ten minutes being sat in the loo, I'd then felt it was safe to come out.
I made my way to the end carriage, which had been almost empty, apart from two blokes.
I asked one of them how long it was, until we had arrived to London.

After explaining that Euston was the next stop and we'd shortly be arriving there, he asked where I was going to.
I think he may have seen through my bodged reply, which was why, he'd had offered me his sandwich.

Unopened it was, and so I took it and then thanked him.
Will do me nice, I probably won't be eating for a while.
And now I wonder, what did he see, in this young kid on a journey?

The train pulls into Euston, and my hearts racing, and
I'm watching out for police that could be peering into the
train from along the platform.
That's if they've put a note out for me, they probably
have I'd thought, I didn't turn up to school this morning.

And still on my back is my books in my schoolbag, last
thing I need are people finding out where I'm really from.
But I'll keep it for now, this backpack is useful, just
avoid the police and I'll be alright.

Keep my head down, keep out of sight, and don't hang
around in the station,
Maybe when I go outside, on the floor, there's a chance,
I'll find a travelcard

But it's still early in the day, and so I make my way,
towards the East End.
I'm soon in Whitechapel, as usual it's busy, but no sign
yet of anyone that I know.

The next girl that I meet, she worked on the street, and
had asked me if I'd heard the news about Joanne.

She'd been put in a secure unit for her own safety, deep down we all knew, it was a probably what had been best for her really.

So she's not around, and in a way, it's like I'm back for the first time here.
I'll make it up as I go along, I've got this far, and something will come.

So I go to the Dellow, at least I have there, somewhere at least that I can go.
I'm not really worried, and for now it all, just is what it is - I'll be alright.

Again I walk in, with my fake identity.
For now I'm Toby Sycamore, a local lad, a true-speaking Cockney.

No-one's gonna grass me up in here, and the staff seem to be buying my story.
They tell me that the police aren't allowed inside for some reason, always a bonus for a runaway like me.

I stand in the yard, asking homeless people if they have a spare cigarette.

Mostly everyone says no, but then one bloke shares.
Another guy in his thirties had been standing nearby,
Tells me that he'll ponse a cigarette from someone and save me half.

He asked me if I was sleeping out on the street, "Not really" I said, "But my friend who I know, she's been put away, and she isn't there."

"I've got a place you can stay", he said to me, but I didn't know who he was and I wouldn't want to intrude.

I thanked him and said that I'd be alright, and floated around with no real plan.
Half-hour later I saw him again, he told me to just think about it.

"I've got a nice comfy sofa and a Nicam TV, and a kid your age shouldn't be out on the street.
I don't expect anything at all in return", and then I said "Thank you, alright."

He said that he lived in Edmonton Green, I'd never heard
of that place before.
The Dellow was about due to close, and so we then made
our way.

"What's in your bag?" he then asked me, "just bits and
bobs" I then reply.
Always trying to hide the fact that I've ran away.

He'd made a plan that we would ask, people passing for
some spare change.
I'm his little brother and I need my medication, and please
could they help us get me home.

But I may as well add a little fun into this, pretend that
I'm blind.
Why not? It's a laugh.

I stare to the side of people he's stopping, pretending
that I can't see at all
A couple of people give him some change, but most of
them don't, and now I'm tired of walking.

He says that he's got some sort of plan, and then we've made our way back into Whitechapel.

He then asks me to wait and stay where I am, before crossing the road and then disappearing off into one of the shops.
He's been a while, but then comes back with a carrier bag, full of blank videos.

We then take a walk round near the side of the hospital, and stop at a bench, before he asks me to go and find some pens.
He already has one and so I come back with another, blagged it from a local shop, I see he's laid the videos out onto the floor.

"I want you to make up the names of some porno's", he says whilst he's holding his pen.
Before going on to write onto one of their labels, in big block letters - 'Fist Fest'.

"Put some Asian stuff in there" he says, "loads of the Pakistani blokes will buy um",

As he writes on another - 'Bangladeshi gangbang, 1, 2 &
3.'

Not proud to say but I had indeed filled in some labels,
and racked my brains, to come up with some names.

Before we packed them away, he'd go on to say,
"We're off to a place called Petticoat Lane."

When we got there I saw people selling their things, on
blankets laid out on the floor.
We'd then been lent some tarpaulin that would work
just as fine, from a guy at a close by market stall.

The guy I was with then laid out the blanket, and placed
all the videos down.
We sat behind them as he then shouted, "three pound
each, two for a fiver."

Men were stopping, reading, asking; the videos had been
quickly selling.
One bloke had even asked "They're not going to be blank
when I get home are they?"
"Of course not mate" I'd then reply, just hoping he did
not live close.

But it turned out he did, and so I gave him my apologies.
"I'm really sorry about that mate, it must be some sort
of mistake."
I offered him a refund, or he could take another.

"I'll take this one" he then said, "I trust your word is
good on this."
"Course it is" I then reply, "Enjoy the films" I said.

By then the guy I had been with, had said to me he'd had
to go,
And I'd been there sat on my own, until near the end of
the day.
Had almost sold all of the blanks that were disguised as
porno vids.
And he came back, sometime soon later, when there were
only two.

We'd waited till we sold them both, eighty pounds is
what we'd made.
He gave me twenty and said I should invest and buy some
more.

Got to his place, a dusty flat, right above a
hairdresser's, just down the road from Edmonton Green
station.

Then he rolls up some tin foil, I've already seen this
done before, smoking smack and he's chasing the dragon.

Joanne would have never let me, but it must be good if
they all smoke it, just once maybe, I'd like to have a try.

And then to my delight he offers, and I accept, although
I've seen it done before, I'm not sure what I'm doing.

I try to inhale as I light underneath, he told me I didn't
quite do it properly, but I'd felt that I'd got just a little
bit of something.

Nothing that I found it particularly interesting.
He went to bed, and I got myself an hour or two's kip
on his sofa.

So on the next day just before we had split ways, after
we'd been back to the Dellow.

He'd once more advised, that I made my way, once again to sell some blank vids.

Written down some dodgy names, got a blanket from the Dellow, then walked back to make my stall, at Petticoat Lane market.

Laid down the blanket, sat down for hours, and half-way through the day, I see the man who's taught me this walking past me once again.

He tells me that I'm welcome back, and hopes that I will sell a few, and make myself an earner.
I've left my rucksack at his flat and unknowingly to me, he's gone and he's looked through it.
Trusted him too much I guess, I hadn't known that he now knew, that I had ran away.

By the end of the day, I've made just over ninety pounds. And because I had ran away, wearing my school uniform, making this money had felt great news, I'm off to buy some clothes.

I head into the centre of town, to Oxford Circus where I'd once seen a big sports clothing store.

Brought myself some trainers, socks, boxers, joggers, shirt and a hoodie, before heading up to Tottenham Court road — to get a haircut for five pounds.

And so later then went back to Edmonton Green to show my new mate, how great the things I got were. Surely he'd be glad, that I sold a few more vids, maybe even be a little proud for me like.

Got to his flat and said hello, and showed him not only what I was wearing, but also a coat that I had brought that I'd put in the bag.

He asked me how much money I had left, "Hardly nothing" I then replied, because I'd spent it all, on getting myself sorted out.

"Where's my readies?" he suddenly said, and I didn't have a clue what he had meant. "You stopped here last night, and if you're stopping again, you pay me my readies, you pay me my rent."

But all I could picture was a bowl of porridge, why did it have to sound so much like Ready Brek?

And then he flipped.
Ripped the bag out of my hands, and walked straight
into his bedroom.

He quickly looked inside the bag, apart from the coat and
my old socks, there was only my school shirt and
trousers, that I'd changed out of.

Then he paced right up to me, with what seems to be a
big machete.
I'm simply stunned, not even sure of what to think.

He holds it up to near my neck, threatening to kill me if,
I dare to make a sound.
"There's no-one around that will hear ya", he then goes
on to say.

He then throws out my black school trousers and white
school shirt, from inside the bag, and out onto the floor.

"Take everything off and put it straight back inside of
that bag, I'm not a nonce so I'll turn around.
Just do it quickly and don't fuck about."

After changing back into my school uniform, I'm greeted
with a machete to my stomach.
And an intense description of how he could happily chop
me into pieces and no-one would have ever known about it.

"I'm going out for a minute" he then goes on to say
"Don't you try going anywhere, if I catch you,
I swear that I'll fackin I'll kill ya."

He then locks the door, no point in me doing anything
drastic just yet.
Give it a moment, he might still come back, or he could be
outside waiting for me, to make a move.

A good few minutes has now gone by, and I know that
he's double locked the door, and so I make my way, over
to the window.

There's a drainpipe almost in reach nearby, but I'm not
too confident that I can get to it, or if I'll fall on my way
down.
The hairdressers below, seems to be closed, and the
street seems quiet and bare.

No-one is there, maybe if I keep looking out, then someone surely will pass along, in just a moment.

A good five minutes passes by, and then I see a lady, walking along the road towards me.
Surely now some help's arrived, this has got to be the end, finally I'm free!

"Help me! Help me!" I shout down to the lady.
"I've been kidnapped, please love could you, just call the police."

She looked up at me, a face of confusion as if she wasn't too sure what to make of it all.
"Please love can you call the police. I've been kidnapped", I shouted down to her once more.

Perhaps she hadn't spoken good English, or understood my accent.
She stood still for a moment, still staring up, before replying "Sorry" and then turning around,
Before walking off further, to the end of the road.

Did that really just happen?
What the fuck, was that real?
I sat back down on to the sofa.
And gave up all hope.
People are shit.

Around twenty minutes later he came back again, and I'd
heard the sounds of him turning his keys in the lock.
What's next? I wonder.
Not too sure what will happen, or if it's possible that
this guy will kill me.

He then came upstairs and whilst walking past, had
looked at me with rage and disgust.
Probably just to scare me, but I had then noticed that he
hadn't locked the door.

How great, how great, how great, how great,
I've seen a chance to make my fate.

When he's gone back to his room, I make a run, and open
the door as fast as I can, frantically.
He's seen me, and after I just make it out, he runs after
me.

Just don't slow down or turn to look, and I might just
end up OK.
It's now or never, nothing to lose, and here's my chance
to get away.

At some point he stopped giving chase, as I heard him
then shout to me, "You're brown bread when I find you."

But his threat had not one bit scared me, as in my head
I'd seen a loaf.

"Uh?"

Two minutes until the train gets here,
He could arrive at any second. Will I see his face again?

He's got my schoolbag, but I'm happy to lose it, and just
be out of there.
The train arrives, and once the doors have closed on me,
I know that I am safer now.

I stay on there until I've got back in town.
And now I am on high alert, but finally I'm free.

APOLLO THEATRE

I take the train from Edmonton, and arrive at Liverpool
Street.
I've got no clue where to go from here, and no socks on
my feet.

I'll go to London Victoria, I'll roam and I'll explore.
This place is still quite unfamiliar, even though I've been
here before.

I walk past a homeless man and woman, and I catch the
man's eye.
And as I do, with most I pass, I smile and then say "Hi."

He asks me how I have been, I tell him what I've just ran
from.
And how I'm now left with nothing, and most of my
clothes are gone.

All I've got is my school trousers, my shoes and my
school shirt,
He showed his true sympathies, and said sorry I'd been
hurt.

"You can't be out just wearing that, when it gets cold
at night,
Here take this jumper kid, I'll get another it's alright."

It was a big thick heavy old-man jumper, which I had then
thanked him much for.
When he learned that I'd no place to sleep, he said
"Sleep by this door."

"You're out of the wind and you're out of the rain, and
there'll often be someone else there.
As long as you move, when the cleaners arrive,
no-one at all here will care."

He showed me by using bits of cardboard boxes, how he
put a shelter together.
I'd now had some slight sense of privacy, and was
shielded from the cold weather.

By day I'd wander through the streets, by night I'd go back there.
For some reason I'd felt more free, than I had in care.
No Longer near Whitechapel, in case I saw that man.
He probably don't come around here, and has no clue where I am.

No-one is gonna take my freedom, I'm happy just to be.
I'm on the street, no food to eat, but nothing bothers me.

Across the road was an internet café, that stayed open all through the night.
It had just opened up, and it's warm inside there, and I know I'll be safe and alright.

I still really haven't slept much in a while, and now I'm hearing funny sounds
So I get myself, an hour or two's short kip, before the guard in there does his rounds.

He knows I sleep out and that I need some warmth, and sometimes he will let me be.
Sometimes I stay up and chat on Yahoo, all night in there and drink some tea.

I can tell some in there are too on the streets, eyes
closed and their heads are falling.
Until they wake up, from their own dreamy fall, wishing
that it was now morning.

Sometimes I would get on to the tube, still exploring
places I'd not been.
So many places with interesting names, and so many
things to be seen.

Still hustling outside the underground stations, or
keeping myself out of the rain.
And now it seems to be naturally easy, to give the Old
Bill a fake name.

The last time that I had slept at the Apollo, it's not an
easy memory to think.
A man had offered me some fags and some booze, and had
put something into my drink.

I was out of my tree but could feel he was trying to put
his hands where the man really shouldn't.
I got up whilst swaying, to try and fight the man, even
though I knew I couldn't.

I shouted loudly as I struggled to stand, "I'll kill you, you peado scum prick."
He then turned around and without turning back, he scurried off out of there quick.

I thought it was best off for me after that, to go and be sleeping elsewhere.
I'm probably safer where no-one knows me, but definitely not where I am there.

So once again, I walk the streets, of the West End with no sleep.
I've hardly eaten, and I want to collapse, never before have I felt this weak.

I don't know why I'm really here, not yet found my inspirations.
Just lost and tired and been trying to sleep, on steps outside of train stations.

THE COACHES FROM GLASGOW

Walking around Victoria, you'd always meet a Scot,
Who'd been in London for a few days, and the rucksack
that he'd got,
Was so big and heavy, but his health did seem alright,
He'd be happy and be chatty, it seemed that he was
bright.

We'd hang out a day or two, share our knowledge of the
street.
He'd teach me how to steal stuff I'd show him where to
eat.
Then after a day or two, we'd go on our way.
But so very often, I'd see them another day.

Perhaps it was a few weeks, a month or maybe two,
I'd see them sat down begging, and I'd say "Hi, how are
you?"

But they seemed a different person, and they had no time
to speak,
A bag of bones and lost his spark, it seemed that he'd
gone weak.

And that is what I think had taught me, that heroin
weren't good,
It sucks your soul right down a hole, not feeling like you
should.
I'd tried to say hello again, but they wanted rid of me,
To beg the money to go and score, so often I would see.

And then I wouldn't really see them, I weren't sure
where they'd go.
Some move around or change their lives, or maybe back
to Glasgow.

But I just hope that in time, that some went back to
who was here,
Before being a slave and wasting life, just for the crack
and gear.

SURPRISE

"Spare any change please?" I ask, to a man passing by.
"Sure" he replied before reaching into his back pocket.
At first it looked like it had been a wallet, but instead it
was his warrant card.
"You're nicked", he said.

So I get taken along with him and his colleague, to the
police station, explaining once more that I've ran away.
Waiting again for the escorts, hours passing and then
they're here to collect me.

Back I go to the children's home, I don't feel too bad
about it, because I don't feel that I've hurt anybody, well,
not intentionally or personally anyway

My mum? Nah surely she won't worry, and everyone
knows I'll be alright, well at least that's what's in my
mind.

I guess I'd been too young to imagine a mother
distraught, the only time that we'd spoken about it had
been in the loud heated moments.

The staff were concerned about where I had been, and as
usual the police came in to question me, and so I told
them in a nutshell about everything.

My social worker came to see me the next day, saying
she had some news for me.
I wouldn't of ever have guessed, what was coming next.

Apparently whilst missing, they'd put a picture of me
with an article inside the local rag.

Over in Brownhills, an old lady whom I hadn't seen for
many years, nor could I remember,
from inside a flat on the fifth floor of a block, pointed
me out, to a man she had been sat next to.
My real father.

They'd been in touch. What great news, what I've for so
long wanted.

My social worker Jill had arranged a meeting, and so we
went to Brownhills to meet my nan, at the indoor market
cafe.

We walked in and found the place we'd been looking for.
And there she was, already sat and had given us a warm
welcoming wave.
We shared a hug and said hello.

Old, bless her, couldn't understand a lot of what she
said, her voice was rough but plenty of spirit still left in
her.

She pulled out a small photo asking me if I knew the
person on there.
It was Lee, a friend from my old school, apparently some
sort of distant cousin, on the family tree.

She spoke about seeing me in the paper, and hearing
about me being found again, before sharing old stories of
how she used to too go to London, with a man she had
once fell in love with, many years ago.

It was an interesting hour, things in life felt like they
were fitting back into place.

Surely soon I'll meet my dad
"One step at a time", said my social worker.

Later that day I'd phoned my nan from the number she
had written down on a piece of paper, to let her know
how great it was to meet her.

That evening the payphone inside the kids home rang, a
rare occurrence.

A man had spoken asking for me, straight away I knew
that it had to be him.
The very moment that for so long, I'd been waiting for.

He told me that he could get to Cannock in half an hour,
and so we'd arranged to meet in town.
Soon I went to leave the door of the home, before Donna,
a lady working there asked where I was going.
"I'll be back in a bit" I replied cheerfully, "I'm off to
meet my dad."

"Wait" she said, "you can't just go."
"Yes I can" I then replied. "No-one's gonna stop me."
As I left and made my way up the road, Donna had chased
after me.

"I'm not going to stop you meeting your dad but I have to come with you, that's how we have to do things."
"OK well fine" I replied, all good as long as no-one, was trying to take my dream away.

We wait in town for a few minutes, and then I hear a man call my name, "Ben!"
That's him, the big tall bloke walking from around the corner.

My face is probably hard to read, but inside I'm smiling.
He seems loose, easy to talk to, and speaks like he knows he can't change me.
Like he still can understand, what it's like to be young inside.

He gave me twenty pounds, and said because whilst I was in London away, he'd missed my thirteenth birthday.

Not that I had celebrated it, was just another day that had gone by as I'd been roaming through the city, trying to stay undetected, and trying to survive.

He wrote down on a piece of card my nan's address and
her phone number, and told me if I was in the area and
wanted to find him, to just ask around.

And after an hour or so we'd parted ways, and my dad
said thanks to the social worker for letting us meet.
Later on, the payphone rang again and we spoke more.
What a day, what a brilliant day.

I guess it was a lot of excitement for me to handle, the
next day on my way to school I'd changed my plans, and
from the bus station jumped on the number thirty-three.
I've only been here a couple of times, so the town of
Brownhills is a little new to me.

I headed into the indoor market, and brought a bag of
sweets from the pic 'n' mix stall. I'd never brought one
before, only the penny-mixes from our local newsagents.
To me, this felt a luxury.

Why not I thought, and so I pick, pretty much everything.
Seven pounds and something pence.
That's a lot of sweets.

I ask around to see if anyone local knew my dad, whilst
carrying with me my giant pic 'n' mix bag.
Took me three tries before the fourth man I'd asked,
had given me my dad's address.

I get to the house but no-one's in.
A few seconds later as I'm hanging around wondering
what to do, a woman walked up towards me.

I ask her if she knows my dad, and she explains that
her name is Kay, my dad's girlfriend and invites me in.
She phones my nan's flat to explain that I'm here, and
tells me that the young girl in the pram is called Kirsty,
and that she is my little sister.

She's friendly and welcoming, but I am wondering if maybe
I should go, perhaps I'm in the way and intruding.
But she insists that it's alright for me to wait for my
dad and stay.

Half an hour later he comes through the door, I look at
him and say hello again.

He's a little annoyed because I should be at school, but
completely understanding.
He seemed to be good at putting himself in my shoes.

He decided to take me to my nan's flat, where we can call
the social workers, and explain that I've been found safe.
Nan had laughed a little bit too, seems we have this
cheekiness running in the family.

They know that I'll do what I want to do, I'm a free
spirit is what they all said, and no-one can stop me.

My dad explained on the phone to the staff in the home,
that I'm all well and safe, and he can get me a lift back
and we'll be returning that evening.
They agree, and I embrace the time I spend there with
them both.

The passing days were spent me bunking school again.
My dad did his best to discourage me from turning up, but
I guess a part of him had also wanted to catch up on
some lost time.

Better I be where he knows I'm alright, than sleeping
rough out on the streets.
My nan would offer me the odd cigarette, knowing I would
only go outside to find one anyway.

Sharing with me more old stories from her younger days
in London, and always going on about how much she loved
Daniel O'Donnell's singing.

Outside on my way from the shop, I spoke to a woman
who'd told me that, she was a police officer and was
keeping a close eye and knew all about me.
"I know all about your running away, and I know that
your nan lives up in those flats."

It had taken me aback slightly, after mentioning it to my
nan, I'd soon forgotten.
Then there she was inside the flat, and I was soon to
find it was the typical Westwood wind-up.

Not a police officer but in fact my auntie Maxine, who
again told me more stories from before I could remember.
I had cousins, her four kids.
Tina, Tammy, Tony and Terry.

I think we were all enjoying the family reunions, despite my dad pleading that I'd have to stop bunking from school to run off to here.

"They'll stop me seeing you", he had said.
And so I tried to slow it down, a little.

But school seemed pointless, never there and too far behind, I don't really understand and it's a lot of catching up to do.

More of a seemingly impossible task than something to focus on, and so I try to keep myself entertained but apparently, I'm being disruptive.

And after every day it gets mundane, writing lines in the hallway.
May as well keep entertained, so I peer through the classroom door window, pulling faces at my schoolmates.

Not your model student to say the very least, some may say it was attention seeking, but I think more than anything, that I was curing boredom.

Perhaps I was trying to fight the fact that I was yet
once more again, on the outside looking in.
Not allowed through the door, not a part of what's
going on.

May as well go back to London, it's calling me, make a
life and have a choice, over my own destiny.

It wasn't long before I was back on the motorways,
hitching rides and making my way back into London.

This time I'll go a way that I've not been before and like
always, that way they won't find me, and surely not in
the one of many cars there on the road.

I'm dropped off on the outskirts of Reading where I
catch a train to Paddington.
No conductor on the train, and no barriers at the other
end.

The station seems pretty quiet compared to when I
often would get off instead at Euston.

I'm back again, making it up as I go along.
Not really too sure where I'll go.
Never a plan and not a clue, what is guiding me, to where
I don't ever know.

Just following my feet I guess, don't even think about my
life, I guess I'm numb, and even *that* I don't really feel.
No answers as to why I choose this.
Perhaps it sometimes feels like less confusion, and more
freedom.

DESPERATE DAYS

No place in my mind that I'm going to, just walking
around, this is London town, so much to see.

Still following the tourist trails, walking along the
riverbank, throwing the odd coin to the street
entertainers, if I have any spare on me.

Sleep and food, the last things on my mind, only until I'm
weak and I'm desperate do I realise, it's time to get some
food and some rest.

Nearly always I can find a way, hustle some change or
pick up a travelcard from the street to get the Aldgate
and go to the Dellow.

But today is just another one of those days, where
everything just goes against you.

I feel like I'm starting to turn to jelly, too tired and
hungry,
What have I done?

I find myself near the top end of Strand, sat near a bridge, and in need of a hand.

I close my eyes getting five minutes sleep, and then lift up my head to ask some passing folks, for any spare change.

One of the busiest streets that I'd ever seen, city people on their lunchbreak, most of them walking all in one direction, like they were on their way back from a packed stadium.

But I had no luck, and only the odd person even seemed aware of me there.
I'm invisible to most of them, and here I don't exist.

I haven't had too many days like this before yet, and unknown to me, there are more to come.

Oh what have I done?
Oh what have I done?

'Surely' I think, in the thought that someone might soon offer me some form of help.

I've lifted up my head many times, they probably think I've been smoking brown, in this half-awake state.

"Please help" I shout out, never before in this tone of desperation.

Too weak to say much else, I just want to collapse and then a really rare occurrence, I had started to cry.

Thousands of people have now walked past me, but after an hour or so there seems no hope.
This won't work.
No-one is listening.

I pick myself up and walk around, pleading out to the odd random person that passes by me.
But nothing.

I find myself in Westminster, I ask people there for help, but none of them seem to understand my English.

The more I think about the emptiness, the tiredness, the more I sink into a frustrated desperation.

I've never been this exhausted before.

Oh what have I done?
Oh what have I done?

I then walk up to Leicester Square, asking the cafe on the corner if they had any food spare, the only thing that he could give me, were his own apologies.

A few places now I've tried, but with no success, and it seems there's only one thing left, that I can really do.

Plenty of shops around, but since getting taken into the police station as a kid for shoplifting, I guess it had worked, and I'm just not as confident to do it these days.

A few places that I could try, but it's getting out of the door without being grabbed by the security, or a nearby vigilante.

By the time I've wandered past Berkeley Square, I spot a newsagent on a small stretch of shops, and a stack of sandwiches, by an open door.

Now's my chance, it's now or never, I don't even feel bad about it, because things have never got this bad before.

I suss out my escape plan and it all looks OK, good chance that I will get away, walk in and grab a big baguette and run right out the door.

"Oi! Get back!" the owner shouts, as I quickly run away. And so I sprint fast down the street, a man sticks out his leg to trip me, but I jump right over - I'm away.

I open the wrapper and take a bite, a gift from God, the best food that I feel that I've ever eaten.
First time in a while, that I'd ate like a savage.
Goes down a treat, that's done me nice, and it's hit the spot.

And just like that, everything seems fine again.
Finally it's took a while but now I'm not feeling so weak, and I'm no longer thinking,

'Oh what have I done?
Oh what have I done?'

GREEN PARK

Been walking around for weeks, and hardly slept in all
of my tries.
I've been sitting on train station steps, trying to close
my eyes.

I hear the sound of people pass, as I nearly fall back.
Having almost fell asleep, looking like I'm on the smack.

I close my eyes and hear the sound of people once again.
Having thorough conversations, as they walk from the
tube train.
It sounded busy, I might see if there's change that some
could spare.
So I look up, but realise that no-one is there.

A lady from the Mercedes shop then came up to me.
Asked me if I wanted, a coffee or a tea.

I took up her offer, was grateful and said thank you.
And the next few days, when I'd sat there, the paper
seller would get me one too.

George, he sold the evening standard, and ran the flower
stall.
And Peter sold papers around the corner, I'd soon had
met them all.

I'd fetch their teas and watch their stalls, when they
needed to pee.
And sometimes serve their customers; back then the
Standard wasn't free.

In the end I went back to the Dellow, but this time not
to eat.
But to get a blanket, and sleep out on the street.

I'd saw there were some doorways, where I might not get
moved.
Any sleep would do at all, there's not much I can lose.

So I stayed not far from Green Park, often moving place
to place.
And go into the local cafes, to go and wash my face.

I'd go explore and walk around, all day in the West End,
Or sometimes stand and talk with George, who was my
newfound friend.

EVENING STANDARD

It's getting late on Piccadilly, and night time has set in.
I go and pick up Evening Standard's, some are from the
bin.
Only from the top though, and others from the floor.
I straighten them to try and hide that they've been read
before.

George, the paper sellers gone, and Peter also too.
So I'll get behind a stand, and try and sell a few.
No-one knows that they are second-hand, as I neatly
arrange.
And after I've lost some sales, I learn to get some
change.

"Evening Standard" I call out, and hope I get a bite.
People will still buy a paper, at ten o'clock at night.
It seems the cops don't bat an eye-lid, this seems to
work sound.
And after I'm there two hours, I've made around six
pound.

Enough for me to get a drink, or buy some food somewhere.
There's Mackie's or the pizza place, up by Leicester Square.

The human traffic is now few, the tubes about to close.
I put things back just how they were, so that no-one knows.

INTERCONTINENTAL

My early days at Green Park, before I'd found my spot.
Late-thirteen and with no coat, a thin blanket all I'd got.
I'd sit outside the tube station, when the older beggars
had gone.
Or hustle for some train fare home, obviously a con.

One of those evenings I was sat begging, on the floor
with a blanket around my legs.
When a man said to me, "Why are you out here? And
why is it that someone so young begs?"

I told him that I was eighteen, and that I'd been kicked
out from my home.
He said to me, "Come on, surely your parents would want
you to phone?"

He then had said, that he would help me get a place for
one night,
As long as I was to phone up my folks, and try and make
things alright.

He then asked me to follow him and said that we weren't
walking far,
I stay on my guard when I'm not too sure, about people
who I don't know are.

It wasn't long until we had got to the place he'd said.
We walked into a big hotel and he'd brought me a bed.

He said "Here's the key to your room, until tomorrow you
can stay.
Just promise me, that you'll phone up your folks and tell
them that you're OK."

So I said thanks and pretended to agree thatI would
phone up my folks soon.
Then he soon left, and so I then made my way up to the
room.

I then walked up on the poshest staircase, in my life I'd
ever seen.
And I'd never been to a place so grand, everything
sparkling clean.

I'd never slept or ever been, in a hotel before.
I made my way, then found my room, and then opened the door.

Two massive beds, a huge TV, and there a minibar.
I'll be sure to buy a room again, now I know what hotels are.

I walked into the bathroom it was the biggest that I'd seen.
I ran myself a nice warm bath and then got myself clean.

It's nice to sleep inside tonight, I'm safe and I'm not smelly.
I'll have myself a nice hot drink and watch a bit of telly.

I'll beg up the money to buy one more night, because to sleep in a bed feels nice.
But I don't know how much rooms in hotels really are, so I went down to the desk for the price.

I waited there for just a short moment, until I saw a lady arrive.
I asked her how much was the price of the room, she looked and said "It's one nine five."

"Nineteen pounds fifty?" I went on to ask, two hundred?
I'm sure it can't be.
"One hundred and ninety-five pounds it is, sir", she said
as she smiled back to me.

"For a week?" I replied, that seemed to make sense, at
that price surely that's right.
But I soon had a shock when she said in reply, "No sir
that's just for one night."

To that good man I would like to say thanks, for the
good deed that he did for me.
And I want to say sorry and I should have known better,
that the minibar refreshments weren't free.

Because in hindsight I now feel bad, and I just hope it
didn't hit him too hard.
Only later I knew of what I do, and how he'd get billed on
his card.

I hope that trouble wasn't caused, for that guy that did
me good.
I'd turn back time and not take the things, if only I could.

I was just a runaway, in a teenage state of mind.
Rich or poor you've shown some heart, thanks mate for being kind.

BACK TO CANNOCK

Same old story, going back, because again I've been
caught.
I'm heading back to the kids home, when there is an
escort.

The good thing is, they won't be mad in the home I live.
Much easier for me to feel that they'll all forgive.

I come back to the same old things, my school life's just
a mess.
Always asking what things mean, catching up seemed
stress.

Still doing lines out on my own, still peering through the
door,
Still feeling that being there was pointless, like I had
before.

Didn't see that life could have been worse, but what was
in my head,

Was "Why can't I just have a life, like other kids instead?"
When wanting food, can't get to the fridge to go and make my own.
And wait half-hour outside the office, to ask to use the phone.

Not that I ever really expressed it, until a day that would come soon.
Where I'd smashed half the windows of the downstairs of the home, and kicked the door off the staff room.

Nicked by the police, and get taken to court, from my pocket money the costs will come out.
But to be fair to the courts, it seemed that they had thought, a bit what my life was about.

Various cautions, a few times in the dock, I'd started to get out of control.
But I think the courts knew, that apart from those times, beneath that I was a good soul.

Guess when the times came, for me to get a sentence, when they had seen me standing there.

They just saw a lost kid, who had just flipped his lid,
and unstable with his life in care.

I still see my dad when I go over Brownhills, and my nan
there too - up in the flats.
And once in a blue moon, I'll meet up with my mum, and
we'll have a coffee in one of the cafes.

But I've not many mates that live in this town, and
there's not much for us kids to do.
So I just tag along, with the kids in the home, a few
times we'd gone to do glue.

I'm told there are some foster parents, who've heard a
lot about me.
Who want to bring me in long-term, into their foster
family.

We're off to meet them, Ann and Ted, in Aldridge, not too
far.
So one day I then take a trip, in my social workers car.

Ann - she seemed an angel, a sparkle in her eyes.
Who'd fostered many lads before, from many different
lives.

Ted - I think he was at work, and then I met the others,
There were three, soon to be, my new foster brothers.

And so it seemed a lovely home, but by then I guess,
Whatever social workers said, I simply would say yes.

So in two weeks I will be there, for now I will come back.
Say my goodbyes to those I know, because soon it's time
to pack.

ALDRIDGE

Last moments in the kid's home, I say my goodbyes to
those living in there.
I know by now, that it's just the way it goes.

I already know I'll be sharing a room, I'm top bunk
because the foster brother that I'm sharing with
preferred the bed below.

Fine for me, prefer it anyway, and they've also got bikes
that I can use.
Something before I rarely ever had, unless I'd nicked the
odd one around.

I get there with the clothes I've got, a small bag packed
and not much else.
By the evening I'd met them all, my other foster
brothers Mark and Darren.

Ted my foster dad - which sort of in a way, feels weird
to say - would come back in the evenings.
After being at work all day, delivering meat to the West
Midlands restaurants.

Things were good, Ann was sound and relaxing to be
around.
Down to earth, one of those people with no time for
needless drama, just realness.

A basic love that seemed to take little effort, and a
sparkle in her eyes.
That's how I remember Ann.

Ted was often there if you needed him, but mainly relaxed
in the living room, after having his afternoon nap.

Darren, he was one of a kind, colourblind, but a blinder
with electronics.

We'd break into the tip with our local mate Alex, wiring
Walkman's, speakers and LED's to our bikes - quite fun
really.

Felt a bit like the American kids in the movies, like a UK teenage version of The Goonies.
Weird kids though we were, broke into the clothes bank, and then a police car pulled up.

The policeman wound down his window, and shouted to us to put the clothes back, but there was a knack.
We weren't stealing clothes because we needed them, really we were just having a laugh.

I'd got dressed up in a shell suit, Darren had put on old man's clothes, Alex, well, we pissed ourselves laughing when he'd put on that dress.

Not really sure what the copper had thought, but we took it all off and then we put it all back.

My roommate had moved out sometime soon later, think he went back to his family, and then Darren came to share with me, when Matt moved in.

DJ Matt, he called himself, from a young age he couldn't walk, calipers on his legs whenever he needed to move around.

Without them, just struggling and grabbing on the
kitchen sides, dedicated on making it across the room.
Seems he's used to his struggle, and always refuses my
help.
Guess we're all entitled to a little pride.

Me and Darren, days out in Walsall, meeting up with girls
outside Mackies.

Just the sort of life I'd wanted.
And now I'm seeing a lot more of my dad.
Now I'm living in Aldridge, only a mile or two now from my
old man.

Turns out that poem that I'd sent off, back when in the
kids home, had won the competition for the under-
thirteens.

I've won a camera and a dinner, in London with the team,
from the 'Who Cares' magazine, and with us two, the
winning girl, from the over-thirteens.

"Don't run off Ben", they had all said, but not once
that day, had it even crossed my mind.

Better that I change high school, it's impractical to
travel so far every day.
So then I do, to Brownhills community school, and my
time there feels quite free.

Sure I get into the odd fight or two, and there are some
of the lads, come on the same bus, from Shire Oak the
other school.

They say they're gonna take a pop, but it's alright, it's
only threats.
Unknown to them, I've heard much worse before.

Turns out in class, I'd got a relative, somewhere on the
family tree, some sort of unexpected reunion.

But I guess this soul still isn't settled, but for some
reason that perhaps I will never know,
London is calling me again.

I tell a friend that's in my class, that I plan to do a
runner, and says that he wants to come with me too.
In me I think, I'm not too sure if he can handle it, and
will he simply be, just a liability?

He's not used to the city, and I know I would have had to
take him under my wing.
But he then begs me, and so in the end I agree.
He tells me he goes to cadets, we'll be alright to survive,
he'll get all his army stuff, and we'll make a Bivvy.

Not knowing what a Bivvy was, he made it sound so cosy.
Until we found ourselves somewhere in Bloxwich, tying
blue plastic sheeting between trees.

Apparently we're just meant to sleep, here underneath it
and down on the ground, itchy and muddy.
Sure we've had a nice meal, from a tin on his stove, but
despite all the nature, I'm getting bored.

We make our way into Walsall and set up a Bivvy again.
This time we're close to the town center, and then I tell
him, that I want to get to London town.

"Are you really sure that you want to come with me?" I
had then asked, after him trying to convince me that's
what he wanted.

"Okay" I then said, and so we headed towards the
station to get on the train.
"If anyone stops us, let me do the talking" I'd said to
him, feeling a bit experienced and all that.

We'd got booted off once, but after a while, had found
ourselves on another train into London.
But having no money and going into the city, this time
the conductor had called the Old Bill.

Perhaps that it was meant to be.
"Don't panic" I said, "Just let me do the talking",
confident that I could get us out of this mess.
Two policemen had then got on the train, we might still
be alright, if I'm on the ball with all my sweet talking.

"We've ran away!" my friend then shouts out, the game
is now up. 'Oh you nob' were my thoughts.
I'd given him plenty of opportunities to change his mind
and said that I would take him back.

But despite his cadets, I just couldn't see him staying long in the city, and nor would I have really wanted him to.
Thames Valley police took us to Reading police station, and we wait for the police in Staffordshire, to take us back home.

Felt a bit guilty when I got back to Ann and Ted's, and after that had never really felt the same ever again.
Despite it all at my new home still being cool, I felt I'd let the side down a little.

And so it wasn't long until, yet again, spur of the moment, my itchy feet had wandered.

This time on the fifty-one bus into Brum. West Midlands police peering through the downstairs windows, looking for somebody, as I head into the city.
Heart is beating once again, surely now I'm not at school the word is out.
And is it me they're looking for?

In my head like times before, I think that they will want to catch me, before I can get myself into London town.

Stash my school books under the seat, walk with my head down to New Street.

But guards are there checking for tickets, I'll have to take the motorways.
Doesn't often take too long to hitch a ride, after another all-day walk, I'm soon in town again.

Back to this place, not really knowing, why I wander, I guess that I just like being here.
Sure, I felt guilty, but I had no answers, perhaps I didn't care enough, or think enough, maybe one day I will know.

I'd not much pondered on my life, autopilot and perhaps numb.

Why I now won't seem to settle, I don't know, and no-one else can seem to probe answers from me.
They've all tried so many times.

My time with Ann and Ted, compared to most was long, more happy than I'd been for quite some time.
Lovely people, and no real reason for me to go.

Just my itchy feet, and London calling.

KEV, DAVE AND THE LONDON CONNECTION

Been tipped off by a homeless bloke, of a place in
Charing Cross,
Where I can get a bite to eat, and a free pair of socks.
I'll go and find this day center, and hope that they don't
say,
A thing to the local police, and know I've ran away.

I make my way to Adelaide Street, walk past Trafalgar
Square.
Find the place and then I see, the entrance to it there.
I ring the bell that's on the door, hope they let me in
somehow,
And after I've said hello, they said that they'd buzz me
in now.

I pull the door and walk up to a desk and then give my
name,
Not my real one of course that would be insane.

187

The police have caught me under Toby, so now my names
I'd mix.
And so I picked one I'd heard of, and now this one sticks.

By now I'd learned to be prepared, and I knew it was
worth,
To go into these sort of places, with a pre-rehearsed
date of birth.

As it was my first time there, and I was on the street,
The lady there gave me a slip, to get something to eat.

The room was full of homeless people, some had fell
asleep.
And at the end, a big canteen, that sold food really cheap.

From the hotplate steam would rise, the smell would
drift on by,
Mashed potatoes, chips and gravy, steak and kidney pie.

Even though I'd seen some people, coming through a
door,
It took me quite a while to suss, that there was a
basement floor.

Down there was a pool table, and at the end there were
some showers,
I'll come back here again tomorrow, it's open for five
hours.

Everyone that came in there was under twenty-five,
And I guess in many ways, it helped us stay alive.

The Scottish Ryan's, Brummy Debbie, Darlo Mike and
Kai,
Took me a while not to worry, that staff would know my
lie.

The early days that I'd gone there, I'd made two new
friends,
Taffy Kev and Scouse Dave, who chilled down Green Park
ends.

Invited me for a smoke, we all chilled down by a door,
Sat down in this doorway, that I'd slept inside before.

I'd stop on by, hang out with them, and get stoned
smoking hash.
Sometimes random passers-by, gave us food and cash.

Ten days or so of us being there, hanging on the street,
Along one-day came a Japanese lady, she was petite and
sweet.

Kev and her had fell in love, and so he drifted away,
And Dave, it turned out he had warrants, and had been
nicked one day.

But this doorway that we chill by, I think that I'll stay
there,
The walls shelter me from the wind, and the air-con
blows warm air.

In the morning I am woken, and when I ask what for,
It's the man who runs the Lebanese restaurant next
door.

I'm in the way and so I move, happens every day,
But as long as I keep it clean, he says that it's okay.

The other door more near the street, from where the
air-con blows,
Was at the back of a nightclub, that they called Tokyo
Joes.

I know the police could still find me, and I've got to stay wise.
But it has been nice lately, to sleep and close my eyes.

Every day I see a guy, put cards up by the phone,
For the girls in Mayfair flats, he always works alone.

I see the odd clash on the street, some pacing with a frown,
Because the other card boys, have taken their cards down.

But Martin who I always saw, he indeed was sound,
He'd always come and say hello, when he saw me around.

And it's been nice, the odd few days, to wake up and see.
That some kind soul, has dropped me down a cake and cup of tea.

I still hang out, with George and Peter, outside Green Park station.
Or go around London exploring, searching for inspiration.

And now at the day center, I often make a friend.
There's always someone to talk to, when I'm here in the
West End.

London's West End

BIG ISSUE

Everywhere I'm walking to, I'm always meeting people
that are selling magazines.
Not on a stand, but in their hands, and late at night
some on the floor all laid out nice.

I'd often stop in any weather, and talk with beggars, and
if my bag was stashed, sometimes they had never knew,
that I too, slept on the streets.

But others that I'd got to know, kept telling me that I
should go, and get a badge, because I'll do well, outside
the clubs at night.

With what they said they could be right, they tell of
drops whilst outside shops, and maybe I need something, a
little different to do.

I'm fourteen now and sitting here doing nothing feels
low,
I know I don't just want to take, my prides at stake, and
I know I can do better.

I'm under sixteen, so I have no ID, which to me, back then
made me feel not so free.
And I'm still counting down the days till I'm released from
the state, so I can fly freely.

Maybe just maybe I'll still find a way, it's worth a go,
and you never know, if you don't try.
So I make my way, towards the river and over the bridge
to Vauxhall Cross.
I see the Big Issue office on the corner, and walk in and
up to the desk.

Apparently they need a letter, from a local day center, to
say to them that they know of who I am.
So I walk back to the West End, back to Connections
where my name's Roy and I'm nineteen.

"Hello Roy", the staff would say, and I tell them of
what I need.
I act normal, then it's all done so easily.

So again I walk through Victoria, and wander into Pimlico,
still learning streets that I don't know, and asking for
directions there.

It wasn't long till I was back, once again at Vauxhall
Cross, where right over the other side the Big Issue
office was.

"I've got my letter" then I say, to the lady at the desk,
who tells me to wait on ten minutes, so I'm thankful for
the rest.
Sitting there on a chair, is an older homeless man, in his
eyes a glimmer of hope, he too has come here for his
chance.

"Help yourself to the soup" the lady says, whilst
pointing to an old vending machine, and so I do, and it's
quite nice, it always is, when it comes free.

A man walks from behind the desk, and calls both of us
that are sitting there, "Go to that room, I'll join you
soon", and so he does, as he unlocks the door.

We learn the ropes - a quick induction, common sense I
guess you'd call it.
No drink or drugs whilst wearing your badge, and don't
harass the public.

I take it in and then he says, "The first ten issues come
for free.

Once you sell them then come back, and buy some more
for 60p."

He takes our photos, to put on our badges, and so far
it's looking good.
Life is slightly changing, and I'm enjoying learning
something new.

Five minutes later he walks in, and gives us our badges.
I feel inside me a sense of excitement, it's happening and
this is for real, a way to my own independence.

He lists the pitches we can use, and explains that
obviously all the vendors want the best places.
Piccadilly Circus and Green Park are taken, but outside
Sainsbury's near Victoria is free.

"Big issue!" I call, to the people around and make a point
to smile to them all, but after an hour of only one sale,
at this moment I'm wondering if this is a fail.

So I guess I need to try, something different once again,
so I call out, "Big Issue, one for one-fifty, or two for a
fiver."

People then turn back their heads, return a smile and share a laugh, I'm hungry but the day is bright, some of my soul is still being fed.

My feet are aching, these aren't selling, I'll give myself just one more hour, and then I'm gone to go back begging, the moneys better and I can rest.

Then suddenly within that hour, most get sold I'm left with two, I make my way back to buy more later for that night.
I invest most of what I've made, and if these sell I'll make good cash, their thick and heavy in my bag, but everything's alright.

Late at night I break the rules, and pitch up at all sorts of places - the people in the street don't care, because I've not hurt anyone.

And at times I'd do alright, but it would often take a while, you've got to learn to take rejection if you're gonna keep your smile.

Or take a punch from coked up lads, from inside a limousine, who call out to you from the road, that they'll buy a magazine.

"Come to the window" a voice shouts, and so I do, I take a punch, whilst they all laugh, their minds are sick, but what else can do you do?

But kick the car as it drives off and be prepared to make a run, they don't get out and so you shout, "You bunch of wankers, fucking scum."

And probably best I tweak this method, because standing here outside Green Park, I've sold only one tonight.

I do much better in the day, as people pass and go to work, and once they've seen you a few days, that is when you'll get a drop.

But the money that people put in your hand, don't buy the feeling that you get,
You know in your mind that it's better than begging, and you feel you're not taking something for nothing.

The money's not great and the hours are long and I
couldn't complain because I'd felt alive.
And at the end of the night, it can still feel alright,
when you've just got enough, that you can survive.

FREE DRINKS ON HAYMARKET

This time I'd ran off in my tracksuit top, with a Walsall
FC badge on it.
I'd walked past the big sports cafe down on Haymarket.

I've had a good day hustling, and I'll go in there I think,
To check out what this place is like, and get myself a
drink.

Screens everywhere and racing car tables, this place was
cool I had thought.
And at the end of the room I soon got surprised, that
inside was a basketball court.

I dropped down my bag and in there I went, and took a
few shots at the net.

Then wandered around and walked up the next floor,
because I'm sure that there's more to see yet.

I went to the bar and sat on a seat, and brought myself
one pint of beer.
I'm glancing around then the barman asks me, "So
what's it that brings you in here?"

I then look down at my tracksuit top, and then I go
straight on to say,
"I play in goal for Walsall FC reserves, and it's Millwall
that we play today."

It had been the first thought that I'd had in my head,
which was the main reason I lied.
Always needed a story to keep a good cover, with depth
and sometimes hard I tried.

"You from Australia?" I said to him, "New Zealand" he
said back to me.
And after I'd sat and brought a few whiskies, he told me
the next ones were free.

"Just give me ten pence or something like that, for the
camera that's there on the wall.
Because if they see you give money, and see me give back
change, there's nothing they can do at all."

Another hour or so and plenty of drinks, I now am sure
feeling the whisky,
I say thanks and goodbye and then make my way out, and
then walk along Haymarket tipsy.

A DAY OUT WITH A CAMERA

Always somewhere to explore, somewhere new I'd not
been before.
Many places I can go, where I'll be, I never know.
A five-pound throwaway camera I brought.
A great idea, I had thought.

To take some snaps of where I roam.
To show my mates from back home.
Piccadilly Circus, Leicester Square,
Buckingham Palace, everywhere.

Photos of buses and London's big sights, some took in
the day, and some took at night.
Street entertainers and around Waterloo, I'd have a
great time, with so much to do.

And then I had got to Trafalgar Square, back in the day
when the seed man was there.
Parked up in his van, selling seed from the stall,
To give to the pigeons, feeding them all.

I wanted to take, some snaps of the birds,
And so I brought off him some seed.
Then I asked a stranger, to help with my camera,
Seeds in my hands and covered in birds.

It makes a great picture, even if it looks like,
I'm someone they'd call pigeon man.

I think I did once, print out all the photos,
But they got lost in this life of mine.
But if anything, I now remember,
That it was still possible to have a good time.

TAXI

Again I'm inside a police station, at Charing Cross in the
West End.
And after they've checked me out and all that, a social
worker I thought they would send.

The police asked me, did I want to go back, but however
much I liked Ann and Ted.
Inside I had felt, too ashamed and guilty, that I thought
I'd best elsewhere instead.

Just causing them trouble, and creating hassle, just best
really that I'm out of the way.
I'm not sure what will happen, or when they'll collect me,
or where I will be the next day.

After a while, the police come and get me, and tell me my
lift is outside.
"Your social worker, said that there's nowhere for ya,
and you're off to your mum's for one night."

Expecting the usual secure-escort folk, I had been indeed
surprised,
To be walked out of the station, by one of the coppers,
to a London black cab parked outside.

Wasn't the first time social services had used one, but I
was surprised that the meter was on.
"I might need your directions, when we get a bit closer, if
I'm taking you back where you're from."

"Sure" I replied, "No problem at all", but there wasn't
much else that we'd say.
I've let everyone down, and my mum will be mad, was all I
could think on the way.

And as we got closer, by now past midnight, and the
meter over two hundred pounds.
I took him the wrong way, because I knew an alleyway,
where I could get out and run round.

"Which house is it mate?" as I'm on my old school
friends street,
"It's that one over there near the end."
So he opened the doors, and I jump out and ran, past
Kwik-Save and then round the bend.

I'd heard him shout, as I'd made my run, and for a long time I didn't turn round,
Until I'd got to the fields, to catch back my breath, and listened out for a car sound.

Then as I was walking, I'm then approached, by a lad around town that I knew.
He said "There's some bloke, driving around in a taxi, looking and asking for you."

"Which way did he go?" I then replied, he said that he'd sent him round the estate.
Not sure where I will go, maybe I'll take the roads, there are no trains because it's too late.

So I take a short nap, maybe sleep for half hour, at the baker's doorway on the corner.
But as it gets later, think I need somewhere greater, and get myself to somewhere warmer.

So I head for the station, the one where there are trains to London, Rugeley Trent Valley - ain't far.
Catch the first train to Stafford, to get the one into London, it was there almost about to depart.

Back on my way, not too long since I arrived, having gone into the bog on the train.
Been the shortest time that I'd been back up near home, and already back in London again.

Not really too sure what my mum had then thought, I'll survive and surely they all know.
I'm just feeling more cheer, when I'm out here, making my own way to go.

WEST END ADVENTURES

I'm taking my old usual route,
From Green Park to Leicester Square.
It's been a long day, and night-time's now here,
And my day on the beg has been fair.

I'm thinking of something for me to do,
I've got sixty pounds now here in cash.
There's guys standing at the corner of the Trocadero,
Selling the tourists some hash.

It's not the first time that I've tried to buy weed,
But more often than not I've been skanked.
But once in a while, I trust a warm smile,
And I see that it's good and their thanked.

But others will lead you, walking through Soho,
And lose you so they can buy crack.
And once out of sight, you know that they're gone,
And you know you won't get your cash back.

But there in West End, it wasn't all bad,
No matter how it sometimes seems.
You'd get some good smokes, from South American
blokes,
And the hippy entrepreneur Europeans.

And I never really liked to drink very much,
But maybe I'll have whisky today.
And maybe a meal from a train station restaurant,
And in the arcades I might play.

I might buy a camera, a disposable one,
And take some photos for back home.
Or I might even buy myself some new clothes,
Or maybe a mobile phone.

Could get a haircut, it's only five pounds,
From the place up on Charing Cross Road
Or just spend the whole night browsing the web,
In a net cafe if it rained or if it had snowed.

I might spend the night, on Yahoo chat,
Being honest I live on the street.
And if I'm so tired, that I am wired,
I'll get an hour's sleep on the seat.

Arm's on the table, head's in my arms,
I'm in an uncomfortable heap.
But the guard from the all-night Internet cafe,
Says "Sorry mate, look you can't sleep."

So I make my way past Trafalgar Square,
And start walking back to Green Park.
But I'll sleep by the road, where I know that I'm safe,
Because I don't trust the perves in the dark.

They've already come to me in the day,
And say "I'll give you twenty quid for a blow."
But I'll make sure I'm loud and shout "fuck off you
nonse,
I'll do you in if you don't go."

I'll roar like a lion, and make sure they're running,
And chase them until they're shit scared.
It's because that I'm young and they think that I'm
desperate,
But my pride is not to be spared.

It was good that an angel once came and he spoke,
With a strong lasting message to me.

"You've got to stay wise, and look out for the guys,
who'll offer you some heroin for free".

And indeed they came, a handful of times,
And each and every time I'd say no.
And again I would roar, but they knew I was young,
And half the time it was a show.

Still something in them, knew that I was a kid,
And each and every time they would go.
Without having a fight and they'd walk out of sight,
Probably best just to leave me alone.

There are plenty of real walking tragic life stories,
Walk past me all through the day.
It's a ludicrous business that's open all hours,
But I've seen the price people pay.

Sometimes I'd hang out in Leicester Square,
In a big doorway by the main street.
I'd try to sleep, but street cleaners would beep,
So I'd just chill or find food to eat.

I'd always meet people, there were no questions asked,
About answers I did not want to say.

Those people were friendly, by now I'd forgot,
That I even had ran away.

Sometimes I would walk, to Covent Garden,
To beg money and watch the odd show.
I knew I'd do well if I sat by the cashpoint,
Because I'd made a load there on my first go.

As always I would be careful to be,
Looking out for the Old Bill.
And if they were coming, I'd soon hide my hat,
Be normal and try to be still.

As long as they don't hear me begging,
Not often a thing they will do.
But my heart always beats, I want luck on my side,
And thank God when they've gone and passed through.

But if they do stop, to check who I am,
I give the same old story I make.
A false date of birth, and a quick made up name,
And hope I don't make a mistake.

I'll pull on my trousers, to expose my leg,
And say I'd been stabbed in the thigh.

I know that it's not what is on my own record,
So I may as well give it a try.

Sometimes they would ask, if I was a name,
That came up on the police radio.
But I just shrugged my shoulders, and said that I
weren't him,
And most of the time they would go.

So then I'd pack up, in case they'd walk back,
And then I'd walk off to some place.
Because I don't know still, if the Old Bill,
Had once seen a snap of my face.

I'm somewhere by Bond Street, still learning these
streets,
And I'm not sure where this backstreet goes.
But after a while, I'll soon find my way,
To the doorway at Tokyo Joes.

Upon my return, sometimes I would find,
People had left me food to eat.
A bag full of pastries or a large cold 'hot chocolate',
From the staff in the cafe up the street.

It's felt a good day, whatever I've done,
I guess I enjoy that I'm free.
Got luck on my side, and not yet found much pride,
But for now this is where I will be.

CHARING CROSS

One night I'd been awake so long, walking by Trafalgar
Square.
Looked at the post office doorway, and thought I would
sleep there.

Assumed that I'd be pretty safe, a police station quite
close.
Connections is around the corner, a pub across the road.

Like always, I'd laid cardboard down, as to avoid the chill.
I'm confident that I can blag, if pulled up by Old Bill.
I took my trainers off my feet and place them by my head.
Climb into my sleeping bag, it's nice to be in bed.

I get some good well-needed sleep, and wake up around
eight.
Open my eyes, to my surprise - I was to see my fate.
My bag I'd put behind my head, was luckily still there.
But I looked to find my trainers, and they seemed to be
nowhere.

"Fuckin scumbag, cold-blooded wankers" I'd thought to myself.
I'd have no clue what I would do, or how I'd get some help.

It's early morning, I walk around, then fortunately for me,
I go into the day center, with my fake identity.

The staff asked me why I had, got no shoes on my feet.
So I went on to explain, they'd been pinched on the street.

And although I had not asked, they then took me somewhere,
To a shop to get me, some trainers I could wear.

It had changed my day completely, because before then I'd lost the plot,
But things have turned around for better, with these new trainers that I've got.

Lessons learned and from now on - although it's a bit of a drag,
I'll always now put my trainers, inside my sleeping bag.

AN EARLY CUPPA

I just want a cup of tea, and get out of the rain,
So I pack up all I've got and clean my cardboard up again.
Its half-past five in the morning, didn't get to sleep until
four.
And I know that another food delivery will need away from
the door.

Once in a while I'm thrown a drink, some crisps or a
piece of fruit.
Sometimes I'm simply asked to move, and I know it's time
to shoot.

Sometimes I'd ask how long they'd be, and sometimes
laugh and joke.
And if I know they won't be long, I'd just try and blag a
smoke.

But now I'll try to find a cafe and get a cup of tea,
Maybe in there I'll have a wash, and get some warmth in
me.

Get this chill right out my bones, and I will be alright.
Got to stop this nose from running, because I've been up
all night.

So I turn off Piccadilly, towards a cafe I'd seen before.
I could see some taxi drivers, as I got to the door.
I walked in with my rucksack and my sleeping bag poked
out.
But there I could not buy a tea, "Leave now" the man
would shout.

"We do not want you in here boy, you sleep out in the
dirt.
Your sleeping bag is filthy, and so is your face and shirt.
Don't come back in here again, you'll have to go
elsewhere",
I left by calling him a prick. I felt he didn't care.

Nowhere else had opened yet, so I made my way,
Back to a bookshop on Piccadilly and sat in the doorway.
Morning workers walked on by and up the road they
went.
I'd begged up thirty quid last night and none of it I've
spent.

I'll wait a little longer, for the cafe down the road.
Only kindness and compassion, the staff in that one
showed.
They've never kicked me out of there, sometimes they'd
give me stuff.
They'd pass by on their way to work, and see I'm
sleeping rough.

I'd often pop into that cafe and go to have a wash.
I'd lock the door put down my bag and take my T-shirt
off.
I'll wash my face and wash my bits until the door would
knock.
I often thought that they would think, that I was
smoking rock.

By now morning is well here, and I'm feeling warmer now.
I always know I'll be alright, in the end somehow.

It's taken me around three hours, to buy a cup of tea.
But this one here really does taste nice, and they gave it
me for free.

CURIOUS STRANGERS

I sometimes wonder, if they really knew, I guess I will just
never know.
Some people would come, with some kind-hearted
questions, my answers were sort of a show.

I'd say I was eighteen, and I was out here because I'd
been kicked out and alone.
And sometimes I'd still wonder, if they'd ever thought,
that I'd ran off from care or from home.

It's not often like this but once in a while, you'll find
curious people out there.
That wanted to know why I lived on the streets, it's a
good thing to know that they care.

"Where are you parents? And your other family?" Every
time those folk would ask.
But in fear of being caught or grassed up to the law, I
never give them the true facts.

"What's it like to sleep here? And how can you feel
safe? And at the night time here don't you get cold?
At the side of the road, out here on your own, you don't
even look very old."

Some would be sober and some would be merry, but most
of them just wanted to hear,
What it was like sleeping rough in West End, and was I
on the crack or on the gear?

I'd tell them half-truths, but we'd still somehow connect,
I'm just trying my best to survive.
They'd ask why I couldn't go back home to live, but to
stay undetected I lied.

I told them the truths when they asked of the dangers,
like the drunk folk that will try to start fights.
But after a while you get a thick skin, and you just have
to stand up for your rights.

I tried to avoid having to lie too much, and I just tried to
simply be.
The last thing I wanted was to tug on their sorrows, so
I'd say I was happy and free.

Funny I guess, my life in the West End, and some of the
people I'd meet.
There was once a woman who'd come every few days, and
play scrabble with me on the street.

I'd met Uri Geller, he seemed a nice fella, although I'd
not told him that I'd ran away.
He said he'd charged up a card with his positive vibes,
which would help bring some luck to my day.

The boxer Chris Eubank would come whizzing past me,
on a small silver scooter so fast.
And so many faces that I'd seen on the telly, would once
in a while walk past.

I'll take each day just how it comes, but it wasn't all
lonely and dark.
I'd always still loved, to play with a football, and across
the road was Green Park.

Big groups of lads, we would all kick a ball, and all
nations would come together,
And I'd always find myself something to do, no matter
what sort of weather.

Some kind-hearted folk would take me out for dinner, I'd slept on someone's office floor.
Some would simply drop me some breakfast, and the next day bring some more.

Always this life had brought me some bright sparks, and only now can I think this way.
If it wasn't for those that had poked in their nose, I wouldn't be who I am today.

And if I hadn't broken some boundaries myself, then things could have seemed so much worse.
You're not on your own when good people connect, Like a gift from this great universe.

THE GUITAR

It's raining, I'm singing inside of a doorway, but with no
music I can't get that far.
So I'll save the money that I can beg up, and get myself
a new guitar.

I think I can go to the Victoria Argos, and get me one
for twenty pound.
And it needn't be, top quality, it'll probably get a bit
bashed around.

So I save the coins, that I can get, and when I have then
got enough.
I make my way back, down to Victoria, where I'd once been
sleeping rough.

It weren't far at all, from the Apollo, I remembered
always seeing the door.
So I made my way, in hope that they'd have a cheap
acoustic guitar there in store.

Flicked on through the brochure, skipped through all the
things,
Found a guitar I could afford, with nylon Spanish strings.

That'll do, it's not the best, but that will suit me fine,
I've got enough to buy this one at nineteen-ninety-nine.

I'd hoped that I'd get one today, it's nearly five o'clock.
I type the numbers in the checker, saw that two were in
stock.

I fill a form, pay at the till and wait with my receipt,
And when I hear my number call, I get up off my seat.

Packed inside a cardboard box, I walk my baby out.
Then I dump all the cardboard, because it's hard to walk
about.

Whilst carrying around my rucksack, with my sleeping bag
and stuff.
I've not thought how I'd store it, whilst I'm out there
sleeping rough.

I make my way back to Green Park, and tune it best I
could.
Try to make up some new songs, not that I was good.

I worried that when I slept, would my guitar be alright?
Thanks to the cafe, they let me stash my guitar
overnight.

Some days later, out there begging, seemed it had gone
dry.
One of those times, when had no food, like when I used
to cry.

But sooner or later something comes, somehow I end up
eating.
I guess I end up stressing out, it's only self-defeating.

After I ate, I got my guitar, thought that I'd jam some
more.
Sat down by the gallery, cap out on the floor.

Didn't care about me making cash, I'd just had a bad day,
So I messed around, with some chords, and made a song
to play.

And because I'd felt so hard done by, been struggling to
eat.
I simply sang what I had thought, out there on the
street.

Had taken it too personally that no-one would help, felt
that the whole world was wrong.
So without really thinking too much, I'd simply had sang
out this song.

"Fuck the rich.
What do they do for me and you?
Nothing at all
Fuck the rich.
Don't want no upper-class bullshit, drivin me up the
wall."

Made up some verses on the spot, and then I saw arrive,
Some long-haired merry retro-hippies, in a group of five.

They came strutting to the music, and then they all
danced round,
I nearly went to change the song, but one said, "Don't
change the sound."

So I simply carried on…

"Fuck the rich.
What do they do for me and you?
Nothing at all
Fuck the rich,
Don't want no upper-class bullshit, drivin me up the
wall."

They grooved and swayed, as I played, and then down coins
they threw.
One took the flower from his pocket, and gave that to
me too.

They all said thanks and made their way, a nice moment
was made.
I laughed at what had just happened, was glad that I had
played.

Sometimes I'd have my guitar overnight, and walk
through the West End,
And meet all kinds of different people, acquaintances and
friends.

Like Bau, he's from Mexico and Paulo, he's from Spain.
Paulo taught me how to play bar chords, important in
this game.

Jamming by Trafalgar Square, the Eros statue too.
Always nice to spend the time, with something nice to do.

We'd sit and play the Beatles, I'd try to learn a song.
Was good times to have good friends, as the time passed
along.

Glad that creativity, is again in my life.
I guess singing is my release, a world that's free from
strife.
To escape from feeling numb, to feel my blood go round.
Don't matter how much noise is there, I'm singing my
own sound.

(Note from Author: I never actually had anything against rich
people, many had helped me out. I was just feeling sorry for
myself. Still, in hindsight, I laugh at this moment)

THE FAMILY FROM PLANTATION

Another morning near Green Park, I hadn't got to sleep
until day.
I opened my eyes, and to my surprise, a kid dropped a food
bag by my way.

"I've brought you breakfast" the young lad then said in
an American voice he had spoken.
"Thanks a lot kid" I then replied, it was a nice way to be
awoken.

Come the next day, the young lad came again, this time
with his sister too.
Again with some food, in a brown paper bag, and once
again I said "thank you."

"That's nice of you mate" I then further add, "No
worries" he then replied.
They both then made their way, so I picked up the bag,
and had taken a quick look inside.

The same as before, a hot chocolate and muffin, that was a nice thing I'd thought.
Someone's done right, in keeping them bright, you can tell by the way they've been taught.

I enjoy my breakfast - the taste of the chocolate, and this muffin seems to go down nice too.
And not too long after, I make my way, through the streets looking for something to do.

By the end of night - or most probably morning - I go back to Tokyo Joes door.
And then later that day, I'd seen the kids again, with their folks that I'd not seen before.

They went and they got me a sandwich and cuppa, from the sandwich shop just up the way.
And after I thanked them, they said that they would probably see me again later that day.

And later I seen them, I met all the family, and they took me back to their hotel.
I didn't stay long, but the good vibes were strong, and they let me have a shower as well

232

I know back then, I was lost in my own world, chaotic as
my life was too.
But you never forget, when you meet the good souls
that make a great impact on you.

Because most of my days I'm just doing my thing, and
watching out for those that see me as prey.
And it's not all the time that you just know folk are
fine, that you find come into your day.

But I'd fibbed with my story, like I'd always done, said I
was nineteen years old.
And that I'd been kicked out, from the home of my folks,
the same old story that I'd told.

One day the mother had given me some money, to buy
myself some new clothes to wear.
And after I brought them, I went straight back, to the
hotel to show them back there.

A brief feeling of normal, away from the madness, you'd
be surprised how strange it can seem.
When you've been so far away, and that sort of day is
now a long deep distant dream.

We kept crossing paths, when I was sat by Green Park,
they all seemed to just *be* so freely.
It wasn't that often, there'd be that kind of connection,
with good caring folk around me.

Always nice vibes, they had positive love, beaming from
each every one.
And on the last day, the mother had said, to come and
see them before they had gone.

I'd just about caught them oddly enough, right before
their cab had come.
Outside the hotel, with all their packed bags, and I said
goodbye to them all and the mum.

She went on to say that seeing the sights, was
something that she'd now forgot.
And that us lot meeting, and them helping me, seemed
worth much more than the lot.

Some tears rolled down her face as she spoke, and then
soon the taxi pulled up.
They put in their stuff and before they got in, all of
them wished me good luck.

I said my goodbyes to all of the family, and watched the
cab drive up the road.
And it took many years, to appreciate, the true warmth
and kindness they had showed.

It's what I had needed, with being only human, and having
kept running from care.
I'd made myself lonely, living like I was homeless, with not
much normal love there.

Many acquaintances for short-lived moments, but not
many that I'd call a friend.
There wasn't much normal, living this life, on the
streets of the West End.

I just want to say a really big thanks, to the family that
came from Plantation.
I'll never forget you four in a million, you're really a true
inspiration.

A big ray of light in a world full of weirdness, you loved
unconditionally free.
Believe it or not, you've etched in a page, within the life
memory of me.

To the right and being transformed – where the back door of
Tokyo Joes was.

Piccadilly, Central London.

THE COTTAGE

The police again, not got away,
Been sussed out I'm a runaway.
And yet once more I do not know,
Where I'll be staying tomorrow.

Another station, different time,
Locked up again without a crime.
But when I'd heard, I was glad,
I was going to live with my dad.

He'd moved from Brownhills, now in Bloxwich,
To a place they all called the cottage.
Now you might imagine a nice old stonewalled village,
But it wasn't exactly a postcard country image.

Behind a solid wood gate, the place split into two,
Uncle Steve lived next door, and my cousin Scott too.
Every time I walked in, I would always refrain,
After hearing the Rottweiler had broke from his chain.

He's had a few people, and made police dogs flee,
Which hadn't exactly comforted me.
My uncle Steve's place, there were tools on every chair,
And his main room was full of TV's he'd repair.

Still going round Maxine's and bunking off school,
But despite that behavior everything had seemed cool.
Then on one night, when I was sent off to the shop,
Instead of buying our munchies, I went to the bus stop.

Got the bus into Walsall, and then into Brum,
Without really thinking, what had I done.
And by the end of the night, I had got on a train,
I'm sure you can guess, where I've gone to again.

ANOTHER DAY ON PICCADILLY

You soon learn the little things, like scouting out your
ground.
You need to see if there are other beggars there around.
Sometimes I'll be on someone's patch, and we'll both
work things out.
Or sometimes there's no time to talk and I might get a
clout.

But usually it's just a threat, so that I'll move quick.
I tell them whilst being reasonable,
"Don't treat me like a dick."
Some will be alright with you, and let you have more time.
"It's alright mate, we share this street, it's everyone's
not mine."

Some will share with you good tips, of good places they
know.
But with some it's just a blag, so that you will go.

239

Some will threaten once they've scored, you'd better be away.
But that kind of attitude, just made me want to stay.

Some just sense that I'm a runaway, and offer me support.
And some will try to take advantage, rob me with no thought.
But not upfront unless they're armed, or I'm asleep instead.
I put my trainers in my sleeping bag, rucksack under my head

Some will keep an eye on you, to make sure you're alright.
Others are the reason I don't tend to sleep at night.
Some look like they've lost their way, too desperate for the smack.
Some will reason with a deal, and we'll watch each other's back.

Some walk past me in a rush, out to get their hit.

Seeing them pace so desperately, made me see that smack was shit.

Some will make a stressed sad face, and I see that it's fake.

But they must be doing something right, with how much some can make.

They're out all day, and out all night, and out in the bad weather.

But there seems no luxury, of being a full-time beggar.

The most addicted have no time, unless it's for their gain.

I shake my head when I see, their blankets in the rain.

Some will walk towards me, as I'm about to get a drop.

Walk up to folk talking to me, stand next to them and stop.

They're asking them now for spare change, I think, 'Oh that's just great.'

To stop folk feeling hassled, I say - "Look, please fuck off mate."

But these are often just the faces that put themselves on show.

There's a bag-lady right around the corner, that no-
one's got to know.
Another street, two war veterans are sleeping side by
side.
And down the road there is a man, whose whole family
had died.

Some will say hello to you, and stop as they pass.
Some have deep rough northern voices, others middle
class.
Some are from another country, an accent I've not heard.
Some of the Scots around West End, you can't make
out a word.

Some are from America, often been deported.
Had some kind of drug charge, and now they're
unsupported.
Their parents one day born in England, and so for their
crimes,
They find themselves alone in London, I've heard it a few
times.

Some have just come out of nick, and some are just
depressed.

Some just seem that they're content, and others always
stressed.
Many women I had met, had been abused in life.
And some days walks a pensioner, who had lost his wife.
Some I see are always here, and some they just pass
through.
And some aren't so clear cut, you wonder what they do.

You'll never once see them begging, instead they will
scam.
They're wearing suits and looking smooth, and seem to
have a plan.
Some have been here under a week, and their energy is
bright.
Some are tired on the floor, have seemed to lose their
fight.

Some have shiny clean fresh faces, others have black
toes.
It's another day on Piccadilly, and that's just how it
goes.

Piccadilly, Central London

COALPIT LANE

Again inside a police station, and asked why I'd ran away.
I don't know, it's just habit now really, but not even
that was a fact that I'd been conscious of.

Without really thinking I'd blurted out that it was
because my dad had smoked way too much weed.
Not strictly true, I just hadn't thought it through, a
quick-fire answer that I was soon to find regrettable.

It was just something to say to get the police off my
back, everyone's always asking me for answers, that I
yet haven't even worked out myself.

Sometimes there are those that don't need to ask, they
just can see something, and they just know, and
communicate, a simple common human love.

Again it was the shame of going back, and only now
eighteen years on, is it something that I've thought
about.

Just couldn't face up, better I be elsewhere instead of
hurting the same folk once again.
And plus now I just made hassle for my dad, didn't mean
to and everything was going great.
I really should think before I speak in future.

The Old Bill went to the cottage, nothing for them to
worry about and they didn't care, with at the most being
the faint smell of soap bar in the air.

But by now I had pretty much exhumed my chances of a
settled life.
All the effort, foster homes and meetings.
Nothing seemed to keep me, from running back to London.

They'd stopped sending the secure escorts; it was
costing them too much.
Much cheaper this time to send a social worker, to me
on the train with a travel warrant.
Quite nice to go back home on the trains though.

Perhaps I'd be more suited in a kid's home they said.
More going on, and one that's in Rugeley, the town
that I had pretty much grew up in.

So I find myself in yet another, what they had called then, 'children's units.'
This one was on Coalpit Lane, I'd heard a bit about the name, apparently was always, in the local rag.

I seemed to settle in quite quick.
Weren't much different to the one before, and even the building looked the same.

Unlike before, right at this time, people's lives were often changing.
No tight crew of long term kids, and I felt London calling.
So back again I make my way, by now it feels easy.

No matter how I'll make my way, I know that I'll get there.

A PERSIAN PAL

I've got some money, I'm walking around, and I go into a
Soho arcade.
I've been there before, when I've done well begging, a few
of the games I have played.

I liked the one where I kicked a football, I guess I missed
the beautiful game.
No football in Green Park, and it soon will be dark, and
no-one's out because of the rain.

The other arcade game, in there that I played, was the
one with a big steering wheel.
Where you had to drive lorries and try not to crash
them, the closest it had got to being real.

And sometimes on there, playing it was a man, who
seemed pretty good at this game.
And you'll soon understand, why I think that it's best,
that I needn't give out his true name.

He sold some hashish to help get him by, at the Eros
and around the West End.
He gave me a joint, the best I had smoked, and after time
I'd made a friend.

He came from Iran and was seeking asylum, some of his
own government were out for his blood.
Someone tried to kill him and in his self-defense, well the
whole thing just didn't end good.

Tortured for answers, and tortured in prison, to know
him you wouldn't have guessed.
So placid and calm, a sensitive geezer, who then showed
me the scar on his chest.

All the way down from the top to the bottom, in the
middle it was two inches wide.
I then shook my head and knew that I couldn't,
understand if I had tried.

First time in my life, that I'd drank tea without milk,
when I visited my friend at his home.
I'd sleep on the floor, was nice to be in the warm,
instead of being outside alone.

And then in the morning after a cup of tea, I'd make my
way back into town.
And know that when I was near Piccadilly Circus, I'd most
likely see him around.

And looking back, I remember my friend, who too needed
form of escape.
And turned to the drink, but I'd like to think, that he's
okay now and has had his break.

Don't know what had happened, maybe he's still around,
making himself a comfortable life.
Was he granted asylum? Or gone back to Iran? Has he
now got kids and found a nice wife?

Who knows is the answer, he'd know who he was, if he
ever read this poem someday.
But just like to the rest, I'd made up my age, so he
wouldn't have known that I'd ran away.

PICCADILLY CIRCUS

Some old bloke's sleeping in the doorway, the one that I usually stay.
There are plenty of places and I ain't the type to go and move someone away.

I find myself sleeping in Lillywhite's doorway, my view was of that like a postcard.
Despite all the walking, I'd never much slept, so nodding off wasn't that hard.

A big mix of different characters, out there every day.
Little Mickey, Irish geezer, couldn't understand a word he'd say.

Just like a living leprechaun, couldn't have been bigger than four foot two,
And a guy we'd call 'crazy Chinaman', because of the things he'd do.

Like start to climb the buildings, and scream out really
loud,
We knew it was his mental health, but everyone's
allowed.

People from all cultures, would stop and have a drink,
Some would smoke some hashish, and some would simply
sit and think.

Some guessed I was a runaway, but once more I replied,
"Nah I'm nineteen, really mate" but some knew that I'd
lied.

Some lived the life that I have lived, and spent time too
in care,
But those that gathered at the Eros statue accepted
me being there.

Good times it felt, for two months, until things were no
longer sweet.
Near where I sat, a busker was glassed, a big pool of
blood on the street.

Could see the vibes around there were changing, and soon
robbed of the phone that I'd brought.
Not much I could do, when there'd been a few, easy come
easy go, not distraught.

I'll go back down Piccadilly, and walk towards Green Park.
It had always felt a bit safer there, at around four in
the morning and dark.

No big gatherings of hardcore addicts, just a couple of
beggars there on the street.
I'm left to do my own thing there, but still I'm careful
who I meet.

The Eros statue, Piccadilly Circus

WAKEY WAKEY SUNSHINE

I hear the sounds of buses brakes, eyes still closed and half-asleep.
My head itches, then I scratch - something has woken me.

I've only been here for two hours, I know it's still early.
"Wakey wakey sunshine", I briefly here a man's voice say.

I'm too tired, is this real or am I still dreaming?
Is this just another hallucination, from yet more sleep deprivation?
I really hope that it is, my eyes feel too heavy to open.

"Get up now mate or you'll be arrested", the voice calls louder next to me.
It's the Old Bill, here to move me on again, maybe I'm just in the way.

I open my eyes, to see the legs of a tall policeman.
And then I turn my head to my left, another is squatting
down with a video camera to my face.

Why are they filming? What are they doing?
Behind their heads, the electronic billboards still play.
Cola adverts flash, and then a black cab drives past.

Piccadilly Circus is quiet this time of morning, a brief
break until London starts again.
Another copper then goes through my bag, and makes
sure he has on gloves, just in the case that I'm the
type to have needles.

I've got no spliff so I know I'll be alright, and they never
suss that I'm a teenager these days.
The copper then films, into my bag, that they have then
now started searching,
before patting me down, and going through all of my
pockets.

The camera's back on me, "What's your name, son?"
asks one of the officers.

I give him some bollocks, there are no warrants out for a man that doesn't exist.
Like often with police, a fake accent if I need, just to shake off the lead.

I was always someone else, born at least a hundred miles from home.
They'd often ask what drugs I was on, and had always seemed surprised by my reaction.

I'd protest at the mere thought that I'd get on the hard stuff.
Sometimes they'd tell me to keep it that way, telling me they see so many stories every day.
I've seen what I've seen but still naive and blind, to many more stories from the streets.

The fact that I'm a runaway, to me is forgotten, for now inside my head I'm free.
To myself and everyone else around me, I'm just another person, and age is just a number.

It's always a risk that they'll just know, and my heart is racing until I hear it from their radio.

'Not wanted or known', often enough to keep them at bay, until yet another day.

Never a camera before or since though, what the operation was perhaps I'll never know.
Maybe I'm not the only one, that's in the West End and on the run.

For now they're satisfied to let me go, other officers nod to them from across the road,
to some men on the floor wrapped in blue and white blankets, over the road on Shaftsbury Avenue.

"Be on your way" to me they then say, that's how it goes, so I pack up my things.

I make my way back down Piccadilly, and to the cafe.
And apart from all that, it's just another day.

UP THE SADDLERS

Been picked up from West End Central police station
yet again.
Not sure if there's a room for me, still at Coalpit Lane.

A bloke called Colin picks me up, and says my room is still
there.
He's just trained to be a social worker, and work with
kids in care.

He asks me why is it I run, always from place to place?
And as I'd then have no social worker, if I'd want to be
his case.

He seemed sound and down to earth, and so I said alright.
And looking back I think he tried, to make my life more
bright.

Colin was a Baggies fan, but now Walsall was my team.
He'd take me to the Bescot, which before was just a
dream.

(Crowd chant)

"All the lads and lasses,
You should have seen their faces.
Walking down the Wednesbury Road,
To see the Walsall aces."

(end)

But despite this, nothing could stop me jumping on a train,
Just on impulse, as always, off down south again.
If I'm kicked off then I guess I'm hitchhiking – someway I will get there.

By now I think me and this city, have a love affair.

NOBU

One day an older beggar told me, if I wanted to do well.
Go ham-an-eggin outside Nobu, near the Hilton hotel.
Next door there was a nightclub, a good place he said to
stop.
In case one of the celebrities, gave me a good drop.

So I take up his advice, and go and make my way.
Down the road, towards Hyde Park, past the Hard Rock
Cafe.
I ask a stranger for directions, and so then take a right,
Up a quiet side street, and now it's twelve o'clock at
night.

People go into a club, and taxi drivers wait.
The paparazzi standing by, often until late.
Usually they're tipped off, and know who they've come
for.
Then they all go running round, when some leave
through the back door.

I didn't always do well ham-an-eggin, but it was
something a bit different to do.
I'd seen Mick Jagger, Jarimoquai, and Chris Eubank too,
Driving his big lorry cab, through the tiny street.
And often I'd chat with the taxi drivers that I'd meet.

Mark Owen from Take That, came and gave five pound,
He said "Don't buy drugs" and wished me luck, and I said
"Thanks mate, sound."

And no-one minded me being there, sat by the post-box on
the floor.
And I'd be the last until everyone left, and then make my
way back to my door.

I tapped at that pitch, for around a month, and then in
the end I got bored.
I guess once you've seen it so many times, you've see it
there now all before.

But there are plenty more places to go, so I'll now just
follow my feet.
And I know that I'm sound, if I don't stick around, in
Soho or near Oxford Street.

Nobu, London

Old Park Lane

THE WELSH BROTHERS

Some middle-aged geezer, who comes by sometimes, said
that I should get a pot.
Because I would make much better money, sitting on his
begging spot.

He said that it was, simply a favour, and I'd just sort him
a few pound.
And so I then sat on the museum doorstep, put my cap
down on the ground.

I gave it a go but done better before, three hours later
or so he came by.
I then told him how much, money that I had hustled; he
accused me that I was being sly.

He tried to get me, then to give him, most of the money I
had.
But just cuz I'm young, don't mean I'm a mug, "Don't
think so mate, you fuckin mad?"

He was one of two brothers that had begged in the subways, at the bottom of the road near Hyde Park.
And then one night, he tried to give me a fright, I'd for once gone to sleep during dark.

I'd been awoken, whilst in my bag, with this geezer now on top of me.
With his piercing voice, tried to leave me no choice, to get robbed but I'd got no money.

Weren't too much I could do, I'm in my bag and he's stronger, he didn't believe at first that I'd no cash.
And so then he searched me, finding no money, but didn't find my small piece of hash.

I was talking to Martin whom puts girl's cards in phone boxes, about it all on the next day.
And when I'd pointed out, the bloke I'd been on about, he smashed a glass bottle and chased him away.

I think that it worked, and despite during the nights, I was still out there asleep on my own.
I didn't get any trouble, from the welsh bloke or his brother, he had then seemed to have left me alone.

I still see them pass, slowly fading away, losing themselves on the smack.
Seems that they'll be, another tragic story, of the one's out there that don't come back.

VOLUNTARY RETURNS

Sometimes I'd want to go back, and when I phoned the
home,
They'd get me to collect a travel warrant, and I'd come
back alone.
First walk past Victoria, to Westminster City Hall,
I'd wait around for an hour, and they would sort it all.

Catch the tube to Euston, and then jump on the train.
Two hours or so later, I'm back at Coalpit Lane.
Brought with me begging money, so I wasn't strapped
for cash.
The new lad there had then helped find half-ounce of
soap bar hash.

His name was Lee, came from this town, that I've grew
up in too.
And from then on we all went round, in our little crew.
With Leanne, Laura, Mike, Corina, and Adam who lived
nearby.
We'd walk round the streets, and then chill by the
streams, doing bucket bongs and getting really high.

Also in the home was Rob, who was a bit younger,
compared to all us.
And despite towards the end of it all, we had let him
have a bong, we'd shielded him from taking our drugs.

Always just wanting to be in the crew, can't blame him
at all really, can you?
When your life is confusing, and you find yourself moving
to here, then what else is there to do?

Running out the home at night, chases from the fuzz.
Teasing moving police cameras, just to get a buzz.
Climbing on to shop rooftops, throwing thrown-out food
at folk.
And duck right down when they'd look up, not happy with
our joke.

By now I was on auto-pilot, just like the home before.
I'd have those same frustrating moments, boot off the
office door.

Again arrested, back in court, for a good few times.
And given many chances, for the number of my crimes.

And now I'm given the version of community service for under sixteen's.
Taken out near Derby, quite a beautiful day, out in the forest planting some trees.

Did it have an effect? Well I think possibly, perhaps for a short while it had slowed it all down.
But I've still been back and forth, from the spurs of the moments, wandering around London town.

THE RASTA DRUMMER

Walking through the West End, it's starting to simmer
down.
Just following my footsteps and wandering through
town.
I see a Rasta packing his drum and stool away.
Many times I've passed him, and listened to him play.

I said hello as I walked past, he asked how was my night.
And I replied, "I can't complain, and everything's alright."
It was obvious to all back then, that I lived on the
street.
He asked me what I'd done tonight, and what I'd had to
eat.

I'd explained that I was still, wandering on the go.
And I'd spent a good part of the day, walking to and fro.
He said he knew a place in Soho, that gave some soup
for free.
As well as with it a bread roll, and a cup of tea.

So we made our way from Coventry Street, not walking
far at all.
He gets the food and then comes back, whilst I'm sat on
a wall

"It's good for you this nice hot soup, it will help keep
you warm in the cold.
But I'm not sure this place would have let you inside,
because to be honest you don't look that old."

He told me his stories, of how drunks will annoy him,
stumbling into him and grabbing his drum.
Of how it makes him jump up, and get his point known,
to not disrespect his things like they had done.

Not knowingly ever met a vegetarian, but it's sure easy
to understand.
That he had self-respect, to not have to put up, with
some grabbing his drum with their chicken-grease hand.

With his hypnotic drumming and his endless chanting, he
really rocked Coventry Street.
And now when I walk from up Leicester Square, it's not
the same without his voice and drum beat.

He was one of those there, before the West End had gone quiet, and it seemed that part of town was a blast. When I had felt there, some magic in the air, but it's not always like it was in the past.

The streets were lined with drummers and artists, and hippies giving henna tattoos.
For sure there was crime, but it mostly felt fine, and those out in town had enjoyed their booze.

So it's nice to look back, at that moment in time, and wonder if I've been inspired.
Because it's me that now chants, and sings out songs of peace, and thanks for that soup when I was tired.

THE CRICKLEWOOD CREW

Another sunny afternoon sitting by the road.
I ask two women if they have any spare change at all for
me.

Whilst giving me some coins, one of the ladies asks me, if
I'm looking for a job.

She says she knows someone that can help me get a job
inside a factory.
It's only packing ladies handbags, but three hundred a
week does sound a lot.

I'd do it if I was able to fiddle my way around the security
checks, some cash-in-hand would set me up.
Turns out that her name is Lia, and she came from
Australia.

I'm eighteen I then tell her, same old story, been kicked
out.

Her friend, she was a London girl, and they shared a place.

They had then offered to put me up, for the night and help me out.
On the way they were to tell me, that their housemates would likely worry, knowing they had taken in someone, unknown from the street.

So our plan was to give them a story, and Lia told them, that I was the handyman from where she worked.
Let's just hope that no-one asks me to help them out, and fix anything.

In the house lived the two girls, a bloke from New Zealand, and another from South Africa.
Felt weird often lying, not only with Lia but *to* her as well.
No-one knows, who I really am.

But all there were friendly, and that's when I was at my first ever *proper* party.
Polish squatters lived next-door, backyards joined together, a techno sound system and a chance to feel London's community spirit.

Half a pill, first time experience, in many ways I guess.
Just being this close to people again, I don't often stick around for long.

Great night it was, and the next day, we were to reveal the so-called truth.
Lia confessed, to the house, that she'd taken me off the street.
But they all were quite chilled about it.

People wanted to help me, I'm English so I should sign on they said.
I feel like sooner or later I'm going to get caught out.
Until I'm free when I'm sixteen, and I won't have to lie.

Although I didn't want to lose touch, with Lia and the house.
I knew I couldn't hang around for long.

Sometime later I tried to find, the hairdressers in Mayfair that Lia worked at, but never did, and from there had lost touch, like I had with most.

But for me, a great memory, thank you Lia, and the crew.

THE GIRL FROM NUNEATON

I'll make my way through the West End, to where I'll
rest my head.
To the bookshop on Piccadilly, that's now a camping
shop instead.

A man and woman are there sleeping, and I've seen that
bloke before.
But there's plenty of room, in this big space, I'll go the
other side of the big door.

I'd seen him earlier at Leicester Square, with this girl
around four hours ago.
I'd not seen her around here ever before, she's new and
it's easy to know.

Couldn't tell she was homeless that time I had seen her,
she's clean and her clothes are well kept.

So I was surprised that I saw her again, down on the
floor where I had slept.

As I go to put my cardboard down, and lay it out on the
ground.
I try to do it quietly, not to wake them with the sound.

But then she sits up, in her sleeping bag, and says "Hi,
how are you?"
And I could tell, straight away from her accent, she was
from the midlands too.

She doesn't seem the type at all to be hanging around
with that bloke.
He's hard-core on the heroin, always looking for a
smoke.

She's new around here, don't know these streets, it's
obvious to see.
Then she asks if it's okay, to sleep right next to me.

So I say "Hey, why not" to the girl, "there's plenty
more space over here."
I think that she seems too fresh and naive, to end up on
the crack or the gear.

She told me was nineteen, and been here a day or two,
Had ran off from Nuneaton town and didn't know what to
do.

I told her I was eighteen, just like I did to nearly all,
In case she might grass me up, and give the police a call.

She said she had some money, to get a hotel for the
night,
"Why don't you come with me?" she said, so I replied
"alright."

We waited till the morning came and took a walk about.
She had to go inside her bank, to get her money out.

We looked inside a phone directory, for somewhere to
stay.
And found a bed and breakfast near Gloucester Road
that day.

We checked in, then we relaxed, and chilled out on the
bed.
She pulled my trousers off of me, T-shirt over my head.

And right then all of a sudden, I heard her loudly scream,
"Oh my god you're filthy, you need to have a clean!"

She said "Please now get in the shower, urgh look your
boxer-shorts — they're black.
And make sure that you have a good wash, before you
come back."

The shower was outside of the room, so I then made my
way.
Looked at my face in the mirror, and noticed all my neck
was grey.

So I washed myself for a good fifteen minutes, and tried
hard to get clean.
I guess this moment was a new learning curve, that
would one day help my own self-esteem.

I threw my boxers into the sink, used the hand soap and
then let them soak.
And then made my way back to the hotel room, I'll make
up a rolley to smoke.

So I walked into the room, and soon I knew, that this girl was no longer there.
The window left open, all of the way, and she'd emptied all her handbag bare.

I waited around for a few minutes, but I knew that she weren't to return.
A positive dent is now inside my pride, and in a small way I will learn.

As I now look back in hindsight, I think I took for granted,
The fact I thought she'd be alright, out there taking chances.

I hope that she had gone back home, I guess I would be glad.
To know she had a safe return, back to her mum and dad.

THE WORLD WIDE WEB

It's nice that I can get into the warm, and I know that
I'll be alright,
Because in Victoria and Charing Cross, there are net
cafes open all night.

Nearly always hustle enough money to get a few hours
out of the cold.
And I'd end up playing, some childish games, well I guess
you would at fourteen years old.

Often folk on Yahoo chat, and if that's what I had seen.
Sometimes I'd walk past their computer, and look at
their screen.

Remembering their username, and then message "I see
you",
And laugh at the reactions, that I'd see people do.

Some would reply "Yeah right whatever", and so then from there,
I'd go on to describe, the clothes that they would wear.

They'd then mess with the camera, thinking it was a hack,
And then I would say something like, "Why did you scratch your back?"

Some would freak out, you'd see them stand up, then go looking around everyone's screens.
Some would shout out, and accuse the wrong person, and that's when I would intervene.

"I'm sorry mate, it was just a wind-up, I promise now I'll leave you alone."
I think with being young, some of them found it funny, but others would then shout and moan.

I'd log on to a few chatrooms, I was older I would say.
I'd be honest that I had slept rough, but not that I'd ran away.

People thought that I had lied, debate it soon provoked.
"You've got a laptop in your box?" often people joked.

For over a month or so, I was then to be,
Speaking online to two student nurses at uni.

One I had kept speaking to, time and time again,
If I remember rightly, I think Emma was her name.

And she had invited me, to meet her for a drink.
So I got me some new clothes, made sure I didn't stink.

Got myself a coach ticket, and then called her from a
phone.
After we'd met and had some drinks, she then took me
back home.

A train ride up to Nottingham, then a taxi up the way.
To where she lived, she had some digs, near where
Forest play.

We lay down onto the bed, but to her inconvenience,
I'd kissed girls but that's all I had, of sexual experience.

We'd shared a bed for the night, that was all, and I left the next day.
And a month or so later, felt that I had to tell her, my true age and that I'd ran away.

Don't really know why, just felt right to do, I guess deceiving like that felt a pain.
And of course she went mad, and she said straight away, not to contact her ever again.

BUSTED

It's late at night and I'm on Piccadilly, and not many folk are around.
I lay down and rest my head, on my bag that's on the ground.

Two lads step out of a black cab, look drunk like most this late.
I thought that it's worth asking, "Spare any change please, mate?"

"We've got no money", one lad said "But come join us for a drink."
Their vibe seemed sound, and so I said "Okay, I will I think."

As we walked down towards Hyde Park, I'd took with me my bag.
They said that they're band was gonna be famous, I thought it was a blag.

Just drunken talk, was my first thought, because people
do talk shit.
But when I got to their hotel, it seemed to click a bit.

Their guitars were in the room, in the Intercontinental,
At least I know they're speaking truth, and not just
simply mental.

We had a jam and drank some beer, and I slept on the
bed,
Of one band member who was not there, but somewhere
else instead.

In the morning they said to me, "Well you've tuned a
guitar up before,
Here's our number, give us a call, and come and join us on
a tour."

You'll be our roadie, we'll make sure you're sorted, for
now we have to go skoot."
So I left the hotel, feeling all good and well, and they
went for their video shoot.

A few days later I went to call, to speak with them
again,
The piece of paper had gone soggy, because of the wet
rain.

I tried to guess the numbers, was it a five or an eight or
a three?
But didn't get through to a number at all, perhaps it's
just not meant to be.

I'd almost forgotten about James and Matt, until one day
I then see,
Two years later when visiting dad's, in the room
watching TV.

I laughed and I pointed right at the screen, as they then
played out their show.
I said "I've met those lads, when I was down London, and
they're proper sound lads ya know."

TONSILLITIS

Winter's here, the cold sets in, I've not often felt this rough.
I'm sweating buckets, seeing things, I guess this is when it's tough.

Can't walk no more I need some help, I'm worried I might die.
But no-one comes to offer help as London passes by.

My throat is swollen, hot then cold, I don't know what to do.
So I make my way over the bridge, to St Thomas's hospital in Waterloo.

With my fake name and date of birth, that I use yet once more.
I don't have a national insurance number, but it's okay because I've been here before.

So I wait to see the triage nurse, to help me somehow,
get some care.
There's a three-hour queue, someone asleep in the loo,
and an old man curled up on a chair.

I just want to close my eyes now, and stop feeling this
hard shooting pain.
But I know that I've got to try and stay awake, in case
the nurse calls out my name.

The hundredth time I've heard the door swing open, but
this time to my surprise,
I then hear the nurse calling out my fake name, as I
wake up and open my eyes.

I pick up my rucksack and get off my chair, and reply to
the nurse "Hey that's me",
I'm relieved I'll get help, because I can't live like this, and
I don't know where else I would be.

"Your glands are all swollen and your temperature is
high, its tonsillitis" she says.
"Just get some rest and drink plenty of fluids, over the
next six or so days."

"I've nowhere to go and I live on the streets" I say in
reply with a puff.
She gives me a flyer with a Shelterline number, that
she gives to all those sleeping rough.

Sometimes I would phone and find a bed for the night,
until the next day the time came,
When they said "Let's go to the jobcentre, to fill out
your benefit claim."

So once again, I make an excuse, and find a way to
disappear.
I'll walk down the roads until I'm back in the West End,
because I'm scared the Old Bill finds me here.

I know that as long as I keep my neck warm, and make
sure that I don't get froze.
That I'll be alright, and I'll heal through the night, I'll
keep covered from my head to my toes.
So I make my cocoon back at Tokyo Joes, and I just hope
no-one moves me on.
But they're used to me now and they let me stay more,
because I make sure it's clean when I'm gone.

I'll drink plenty of liquids and maybe some whisky, because
I was told that it warms your inside.
After just a few days I'm out of the haze, and my
swollen necks now not as wide.

I'm nearly back to myself and I'm glad that it's nearly
gone, felt like I was dying, but now I'm alive.
Still not a hundred percent, but at least I'm not dead,
and I'm just glad that I will survive.

CHRISTMAS

Is there any point of going back? I know what it will be.
Just me and maybe one more kid, there's not much there
to see.

Last time that I did Christmas day inside the children's
home.
It was just me and one of the staff, spent most of the
day alone.

Most of the kids returned to their folks, to share with
them their Christmas day,
But in my lost world, I don't question a thing; I think
there's not much I can say.

So this Christmas, I ain't going back, I'll stay instead in
London town.
It's only Christmas, all I'm missing is the dinner, and it's
not something that gets me down.

For sure I'm thinking of family at home, and hope that
they have a nice time.

My mind says by now, they think I'll be okay, because I've
so often turned back up fine.

I know there'll be others sleeping rough on the streets,
especially more deep in the West End,
I can't see that I'm numb, spending Christmas alone, not
even sat with a friend.

Piccadilly's footpaths have gone quiet, and even the road,
which is rare.
But the weather's been pleasant, it only rained for a bit,
and there's a cool breeze in the air.

I've taken a wander around the West End, and returned
back to my spot.
And no-one's moved the cardboard I'd left, so I lay
everything down there and plot.

I'll read a leaflet, magazine, or maybe sing a song,
Always think of something, to help pass the time along.

Not many pass but those that do, acknowledge that I'm
there,
We both say "Merry Christmas", a brief nice moment
that we share.

Later when the night kicks in, more come into town.
The merry folk will stop and joke, and drop a beer down.

They will often stop and talk with me, and some will
offer me some change.
Again it's always the bright faces that stop life feeling
strange.

The night has ended, the next day isn't so quiet, and
there's people go out for their walks.
Another usual day of meeting plenty of strangers, and
finding myself in some talks.

With all sorts of people from rich folk to the homeless,
the Christmas spirit still in the air.
Could you really blame me, for wanting to be, here more
than a place that was bare?

NOT QUITE LONDON

It must have been a full moon, I reckon, or something.
Ten o'clock had gone and the staff had asked us to all
go into our own rooms.
With it being a Friday night, none of us had wanted to.

The lady working the waking night shifts often accepted
our youthfulness; usually she had being quite lenient.
But with Kath, who was sleeping in asking us all to go
to bed, she had to play the part.

But instead of the expected calm, things had only become
more erratic.

The sounds of doors slamming, from across the halls,
and conversations at various volumes.
None of us were listening to the staff members requests,
and so then, the police were called.

One policeman came upstairs, whilst another had been
having stern words with Lee, down below.

Leanne had been in my room, whilst I was on the landing. With us being different sexes, they wouldn't let us hang out together in each other's rooms.

I'd returned whilst the policeman was busy pushing Michael back into his room, and then me and Leanne had decided to barricade ourselves in.

Far from the best of barricades, when the policeman had got his other colleagues, the door was pushed ajar, and he'd managed to climb over it.

Once he was inside, he opened the door, making a firm point of telling me to stay in my room for the night, and not come out, unless I needed the toilet.

I hadn't been the only one, to answer back, his thoughts were probably that pinning me up against the wall might teach me a lesson, or make me think twice the next time.

"Do you think that was hard do ya, you fuckin bully" I said before he'd launched towards me.
And so I ran and locked myself in my room, which was most likely what he had intended.

Sure we were all a bit of a handful, but with us all in our rooms, the staff now had peace.

But this is Coalpit Lane,
And peace is just a moment.

. . .

Fifteen minutes or so later, once we'd all started to hear each other's voices from across the hallways, one by one we were all back there on the landing.

Michael was running around whilst screaming, with a duvet wrapped around him, smoking a cigarette, which wasn't allowed.

Me, well I was messing around and lighting small bits of tissue paper to set off all of the smoke alarms. Not really sure why, and you should know that I'm not proud.

Everyone else had been floating about, or sitting down on the landing floor.

The staff weren't happy at all.

I think a lot of us had maybe felt, a bit distant to Kath compared to some of the other staff that had worked in our home.

It felt that for whatever reason she hadn't broke through to know us that well, and it seemed her work life was more office-based, than being around all us lot. Something else major was probably going on in her life.

Maybe it was part of the reason, the slight sense of miscommunication, that Michael hadn't thought twice about doing what he'd done next.
I myself was slightly taken aback when it had happened.

Without seemingly much thought, Michael threw his duvet over Kath.
I could see she had panicked, whilst trying to get it off herself, but had only got caught up in it worse.

I pulled the blanket away, to try to help get it off her. And after that I'd sort of lost the plot a little, and foolishly, may I add.
In a moment of my own madness, I had set fire to some tissue paper, in the card-phone room.

Without even thinking of the consequences, I'd wanted to set off all of the alarms, and fill the small room with the smoke.

Of course I now know, in hindsight looking back, that it wasn't a well thought out joke.

I knew that the fire would be somewhat contained, and that the carpets were fireproof standard.
But I was being a loose-cannon, and I had highly underestimated what I had done.

Whilst the fire alarms were all going off, one of the kids had led the staff, to where I'd lit the fire.
As they opened the door, the rest of the hall had filled up with smoke.

Immediately then, I knew that I'd taken it all too far, the fire brigade then came, and also the police.

Apparently I'd burnt right through the fire resistant carpet. A lucky escape for everyone, to not have set fire to the front of the house.

It was under the recommendation of the fire brigade to the police that I be charged.

And so then on that Friday night, I was arrested and later charged, for arson with intent to endanger life.

The police had told me that this was indeed serious, and I could be looking at a few years, inside jail.
My world was spinning, in a hole I am falling - I'd well and truly fucked it all up.

The complete opposite of what I'd always wanted.
Locked away for years? I just couldn't quite come to terms with it all.
I'll be in my twenties when I am released.

Oh what have I done, Oh what have I done?

After being moved to another police station on the Sunday, on Monday morning I was then taken to court.

It had been referred straight to a crown court trial, and after being denied bail I was taken to Stoke Heath Young Offender's Institute.

I'd heard about it a few times before, people saying it had been on the TV, and inmates were getting thrown boiling hot and sweet water into their faces.

I hadn't known what to think, just deal with things as they come, not to say I wasn't bricking it.

The van had driven from prison to prison, me and one lad, we were the last, and it didn't seem too bad getting out of the 'meat wagon', nice weather and that.

Quite a nice stroll, walking through the yard and into the entrance, unknown to me then that a few moments later I'd be squatting naked with my legs open, and lifting my balls to prove that I haven't smuggled anything into jail.

After changing into her majesty's pleasures clothing range, and given a pack of odds and ends, I'd just about got there in time, to join the end of the dinner queue.

The food was alright to be fair, but don't ask me what it was, because I can't remember.

It had been a quiet night I guess, and at the time unknown to me, the next day Colin, my social worker, would come to take me to a secure unit.
Six weeks on remand, but still, it's better than jail.

The secure unit was on the edge of Derbyshire, and Colin assured me that I'd be alright.

Apparently it wasn't much different from being in a kid's home, except in there is a school, and obviously I wouldn't have been able to get out.

And soon we arrived to a pentagon-shaped, dark-red bricked building with tall walls around, and drive into a garage where the door shuts behind us, before we'd got out.

I'd been expecting a more clinical induction, it was clear that I was most likely going to have to be strip-searched.

But instead of a uniformed screw-type that I'd expected, I was greeted by a cheerful lady, who said I quickly just

had to go into a room just wearing my pants and then quickly turn around.
Nothing like jail.

I'd expected to be signed in and then put straight into a bedroom, but instead the lady gave me a tour of the whole building.

Each door to every section of the building had coded locks, but instead of feeling like a psychiatric ward, it felt like I'd been walking around some sort of newly built community center.

My eyes lit up when I found out we had a pool table there in our section.
The unit had been split into parts, all named after historic places, not too far.
And between them was the school section, where I peered into a room, to see two kids were doing their work.

I then got shown my room, it looks quite nice, and loads of space in there for me.
Everything rounded and slightly plastic looking, but it certainly could have been much worse.

A bed, a table, and somewhere to put my clothes, as long as I'm happy I'm free.

And then I'm shown the best thing ever - my en-suite shower, big enough to walk into, and was pretty well ventilated.

The smell of fresh linen.
A very clean place, much better than prison.

Despite the only access to the outside world was whilst visiting the doctors, I'd relatively enjoyed it there, and what would happen to me during my upcoming trial, just hadn't been there on my mind.

Sure I'd thought about escaping, but everywhere has cameras, but if I really wanted to, I knew it could be done. However, perhaps I was somewhat content for the time being.

Six weeks passed by, and it was looking like things were going to be alright - and that I wasn't actually going to receive a custodial sentence.

My charges were reduced to criminal damage by fire, but I was to find out soon later that I had also been charged for common assault.
Accused by Kath of holding her down, in the duvet along with Michael.

However, I didn't worry, I'm sure it all will get cleared up. I'd been arrested for a few things in my teenage years, but never once assault.

After having spent my sixteenth birthday inside of the secure unit, it seemed that social services hadn't legally needed to look after me anymore, now that I'm sixteen.

And at the start of my trial, I was released on bail, for just under two weeks, until I was due to return.

I'd been surprised to find that my mum, had put herself forward, to let me use the house as an address for my bail. Something that I hadn't at all expected, until I had heard it in court.

I'd been away from my mum a while by now, perhaps she had been missing me?

The two weeks that I'd spent at home seemed nice, a breath of fresh air, and we all seemed to be getting along.

Things had started to somewhat settle down, and it was looking like that instead of going to jail, that I'd be getting some sort of community service.

Mum had felt confident that this time I'd be lucky, and this was my big lesson, and I'd have a close shave with the courts. Which is why she would joke, about me getting bummed in the showers by a big hairy bloke.

Things had felt great, and it was the first time in a long while that I'd been content at home, and not feeling in limbo.
And so then the first day of the trial came, and I was back inside crown court.

Despite pleading my innocence to my solicitor that I hadn't actually pulled the duvet down over Kath, but instead had pulled it off to help her,
He'd convinced me that it would be best to plead guilty to the charge of assault and he would get them all reduced.

Assuming that he knew what was best for me, I simply agreed, and followed his lead.
However, everyone knew the fire could have easily have got way out of hand, and I'd been expecting the courts to want to send me a serious message.

It wasn't the first time that I'd been messing around with fire.
I'd also been arrested and taken to court only a few months before, for setting fire to a postbox, on one of the streets, just down the road.

I'd already then, had a close brush with the law, with it being the Queen's property and all that.
Perhaps this time I'd get community service?

But there's still a chance that I might not be walking out, the same way in which I had come in.
I walked into the court, dedicated on letting them see my better side, and had taken the trial very seriously indeed.

Michael however, wasn't facing my sort of charges, to him it didn't matter if he joked and smirked during the case, appearing as if was untouchable.

Even I'd been shocked in the way that he had behaved in court, especially as *my* freedom was on the line.
So as he had been sat next to me, I'd elbowed him, and told him to shut the fuck up.

It sort of worked, a little bit, but not completely.

On the next day came sentencing, and if I remember rightly, despite still being confident people would see that I had now learned from my mistakes, I knew Michael's cockiness and bravado in the court, would somehow make an impact on both of our punishments.

We stood up for the main judge, to receive both of our sentences.
Still in serious-mode I remained calm, completely unsure of what will come next, Michael, well he's still smirking, thinking it's all a game.

He had also been charged with some other stuff, nothing at all to do with me, and the judge went on to explain the seriousness of our charges.

First came Mike's, and he received a four-month detention and training order, which had meant he was to do two months inside of a Young Offenders Institute.

Everything about his demeanor changed, there and then he turned bright red, and had burst into tears.

I'd felt a little sorry for him, but another part of me thought that perhaps it had been well overdue, him being taken down a peg or two.

In a small cruel sort of way, I enjoyed seeing it, after the way he'd showed me up in court. And so then he was handcuffed and led off by the security, sobbing along the way.

'Serves you right, for being a cocky twat' I'd thought. From that moment on, I knew that I too would be getting a sentence.

And so I did.

An eight-month detention and training order, which had been reduced down to six, because of the time I'd spent in the secure unit on remand.

I was, to say the very least, quite gutted, but somehow in my own way I'd been prepared for it to happen.
Some sort of acceptance.

Neither my mum nor I had expected it though.
And so I was led, also in handcuffs, by the security officers into the back room, where I was with Michael.

He hadn't handled it well at all, and I tried to assure him that he'd be alright, and to not worry, but he seemed to be in complete total shock.

And so not too long after, we'd got driven off, to Werrington Young Offenders.

Somewhere near Stoke-on-Trent, where I would spend the next three months, and Michael would spend two.

WERRINGTON

Dropped off in the prison van, here's where I'll be.
Mike's in here for two months, and I'll be here for three.
I think I know what to expect, but it's different, alright.
To spending three months here inside, than spending just one night.

The same as when up at Stoke Heath, a strip search then a change,
Into her majesty's pleasures, fashion clothing range.
I see Mike again and we're led to the block, and we're the few that seem new to this thing.
And so we go in, we're we'll be for two weeks, inside the induction wing.

Because Mike was my co-defendant, they put us both in the same cell.
Despite him first crying for most of the night, I told him that things would go well.

After time he seemed to get used to it all, and I guess it
was the same for me.
And then two weeks later, we're moved to the proper
section and we're in wing B.

Now I've got my own cell, which had been number thirteen.
Just like the induction, you get your pad inspection, to
make sure that everything's clean.

First days were boring until I'd started working, in the
kitchens cooking food.
And sure inmates will test ya, and guards will molest ya,
by slapping your arse and being rude.

Never short of a vampire, to try and steal your power,
People claiming they will do ya, when you're in the
shower.

One day a screw opened the door, whilst I had faced the
wall,
Running a sink and machines on, couldn't hear much else
at all.
I'd got done in right from behind, no chance and stars I
saw.
But life's too short, so carry on, just like I did before.

It's not forever, could be worse, and I am quite glad.
That I've had the odd few visits, and got to see my dad.
But contrary to popular belief, a myth that wasn't true.
The one's that had the Nintendo, were the very few.

The alpha males, the wing top dogs, their cells would look like shops.
The currency we traded in, were phone cards and Radox.
And then as the time passed, my final week, and I leave soon.
I've got no clue where I'm going to, or even if I'll find a room.

I'm then released, and picked up by Colin, finally now I am free.
And later on, I'm taken to Stafford, to check into a B&B.

THE FIRST TRUE TASTE OF BEING SIXTEEN

It's nice to be free again, but the next few days had felt
somewhat lonely.
Guess it's nice to have a room, but what is there to do?
Despite running away before to Stafford, I've never lived
here, or really knew it all that well.

Fortunately, a week or so later, I'd got referred to the
YMCA, and I think it had made my mum feel somewhat a
bit proud to see me flying the nest.

For the next month or so, I was to share a flat with
another bloke, who I never really saw that much.
Soon one of the single flats had become available for me.
I'd finally got my independence,
What I had been looking for.

Soon I was happy with my little flat there, and it was
nice to feel that I have a home, but I sort of hadn't
expected, how things would then pan out.

What started from a handful of folk that I vaguely knew from around town, turning up for a spliff or two, had suddenly become a loud party place, where scores of people I didn't even know had turned up.

Perhaps I'd been somewhat vulnerable, with around thirty people crammed into my flat, by then surely it had been, completely taken over.

Then came the news that my nan had passed, it had been a shock not knowing that she hadn't been so well. But I'd thought during that time, I was dealing with things alright.

And then came her funeral day, where I was due to meet my mum, beforehand in the morning.

Without even thinking why, I left my flat door open wide, and headed straight for London.

I lived on the streets again for a while, but this time everything about me, just felt completely different, this ain't cool, and it's not the same no more.

WORTH CALLING

I guess it's taken me a while to feel and truly see.
This way I live and where I sleep, ain't where I should be.
Other kids are leaving school, girlfriends by their side.
And when they see me on the ground, I start to feel my
pride.

I hide my head in sense of shame - it makes me feel low.
I should be home and being with friends, but most now I
don't know.
I'm growing up but what into? I need to find a way.
So I go into the day center, to get some help that day.

The staff knew me but thought that I was nineteen and
called Roy.
So I tell them that for the two years they knew me I
was a boy.
They laughed a bit and said to me that they'd suspected
something there.

And then I go on to explain, I'd been running off from care.

"I've had enough now of the streets" I'd mentioned to the staff.
"I need to make some sort of life, and find some sort of gaff."
They said they knew there of a place, by the river down in Vauxhall.
So then they put me in a referral, to get me into the hostel.

The youngest there well nothing's changed, that's just how life has gone.
It's nice these days, no need to lie, of where I have come from.
No need to make me no fake names, or speak a different voice.
It was always to stay undetected, rather than by choice.

Roughly thirty rooms in there, but I was one of five,
That knew to smoke the brown or white, was no way to be alive.

Sure we'd sometimes share a spliff, and relax with some
tunes.
Our little crew was often found, in each other's rooms.

I'm not sure where my life will go, or what roads lay
ahead.
For now I've got three meals a day, and sleeping in a bed.
I'm still signing in and out, just like I was in care.
No visitors allowed in my room, but at least I have
somewhere.

Every week a guy would come, and his name was Mark.
He'd take us out to play football, in the five-a-side park.
We'd once played the homeless football league, and I
would go in goal.
All the exercise and the fresh air, felt a good thing for
my soul

Some teams they looked intimidating, but we pushed on
to.
And we didn't do half-bad, our little motley crew.
An African lad that was on our team, he could sure run
fine.

And our scrawny mate on heroin, scored from the halfway line.

One day my friend, his name was Liam, I'd seen in frustration.
The lad next door, half hour before, had stolen his PlayStation.
We told the staff but no police came, we didn't understand.
So, I and another one of our mates, took matters into hand.

We'd forced our way into the room, but the Playstation just weren't coming back.
The lad that had nicked it had climbed in through the window, and gone and sold it for some crack.
The mate I was with, gave the lad a smack, he dropped down like a sack of spuds there.
But I'd thought to myself 'bet the pricks used to it', He'll go on like normal, ain't fair.

So being a young youth and wrapped up in the moment, guess I'd once again took it too far.

All night outside the lads room, and I tried to get in,
whenever his door was ajar.

For some strange reason, I'd then decided, to throw wet
tissue when he'd try to come out.
But loads had stuck to his door, and around his
doorframe, and then the staff asked what this was
about.

They had then kicked me out, for a whole seven days and
nights, and I didn't have a clue where I'd stay.
So I asked the staff, if I could have a bit back, of the
service charge that I would pay.

But nothing at all, and whilst I'm outside, the fact
they're still claiming money feels bleak.
Especially when I know the rent their receiving, for me is
two hundred per week.

So with nowhere to go, I then go back to the doorstep,
after a short wander around.
I'm no longer wanting to be on the streets hustling, and
sleeping out down on the ground.

"Can you move on please, Ben" one staff member then
said, before threatening that he'd call the Old Bill
If he hadn't of threatened, I maybe just might have
moved, but it just made me want to stay there more still.

"Please call the police then" I then replied, "I'll tell them
how you're still taking my money."
And it just wound me up, when he looked at me like a
mug, so I said, "Mate, you think this is funny?"

I'd never once been in an activist scene, or been to a
protest before.
But on the streets, walking through town at night, a
few times I wandered past Brian Haw.
With his protest signs, about the wars in Iraq, that I
then had knew nothing about.
So I said to myself, 'if you're still taking my money, then
I'm going to get up and shout'.

So I went to the phone box and rang several big papers,
saying that there had been a demonstration.

To do with the hostel, and with hundreds of people,
filling the street and the inside of the station.

Ran back to the hostel with pieces of cardboard, and
scrounged a few pens on the way.
Then had written out signs, whilst my mates threw out
candles, and the staff once again said I couldn't stay.

I kept my eye out for reporters, but none did I see.
And in the early hours came out the staff, sometime
around three.
He said head office had called the hostel, he's been on
the phone all night.
They have to let me sleep there now, I'm back in and I'm
alright.

But the arranged agreement was, that I was to be
leaving,
Early every morning, can't return until the evening.
So once again I walked the streets, and even then slept
out.
And now it feels like the old days, wandering about.

PSYCHEDELIC

Been at the hostel through this festive season, and now
I'm back in town.
But tonight I'll sleep on Piccadilly, with my sleeping bag
put down.

Not sure why I sleep outside still, I try to get away.
Guess it's nice to meet some different people every day.

Many cars are driving past, and one catches my eye.
And I remember thinking, 'What's all that stuff inside?'

The back seat had been piled with stuff, and then my
thoughts had changed.
And despite me still having a room, being back here didn't
feel that strange.

I got my hat, and got my coat, I guess that I'm used to
the cold.
And at least this winter I've had no tonsillitis, like I did
at fourteen years old

Cars still drive past but it's reasonably quiet, as it's
the next weekend after new year.
But this is the West End, and this place never shuts,
there's always folk out for a beer.

Not too long later I see, a dreadlocked man walk by me,
And like all I say to him "Hello",
He said he had a squat, and it'd be a warm place to plot,
And they were having a party, so I thought I would go.

We got to some old indoor railway arches, just down by
Liverpool Street.
A crew of Columbians, Venezuelans, Brazilians, were some
of the people I'd meet.

And then came Saturday when things had got busy, big
equipment and lots of decor.
This seemed a lot bigger than when I'd been to a
nightclub, with Phil and Trixie from the hostel before.

I'd accepted to help run the bar for the night, as the
techno sound system there played.
All night I had thought, that where I had been, was the
only part of the rave.

And so I went for the toilet, quite a few hours later, and
I was then surprised to see,
That the other arches which I'd thought were empty,
were full to the brim completely.

Strobes and green lazers, hippies with chillums,
And Psy-Trance being played really loud.
The smell of Nag Champa, and it took forever, for me to
get through the crowd.

I'm part of a crew now and every weekend, we host
hundreds in through the squat door,
And I'm now meeting people, on a completely new level,
deeper than I have done before.

THE
END

EPILOGUE

After sticking around with the multicultural mix of squatters over the next three or four years and helping them to make vibrant squat parties across London, Ben continued his interests in playing guitar and singing and eventually dedicated much of his time to songwriting and busking (Live street performance), as well as being the creator of Laughing Beader Bracelets, and having strong interests on various social issues.

Since coming of age, Ben has managed to steer clear of the youthful peer-pressures that had once misguided him, and has since managed to stay out of trouble with the law.

Ben has made various solo acoustic performances around the UK, as well as experimenting with a mix of genres hosted online at sites such as www.fractalmoon.bandcamp.com

In 2017 he dedicated most of the year to writing this book.

NOTE FROM THE AUTHOR

BEN WESTWOOD

If you've made it this far through the book, then thanks for reading, and I hope you've enjoyed it.

Sorry that you've had to put up with a lot of swearing, but without it, you really wouldn't have been there.

If people were to ask me what messages this story puts out to the world, I'm not sure what my answer would be. I guess that's down to the individual reading it.

As for the comedic tones, well despite after many years, coming to realise that it's quite a sad story, I wouldn't have made it this far feeling too sorry for myself.

In a way, the message isn't about me - it's about a young boy, that happened to be me.
I may seem to reel off my own stories effortlessly, but please make no mistake, that I feel for any parents whose child has ran away, and fear for those young and missing.

But as for my story personally, I don't want people to feel sorry for me.
I just want them to see the power they hold within themselves to make an impact around them.

The power through simple actions to transform others days, or even lives.

To step out of the box, and create magic and change. And to never give up, on ourselves or on others.

It's important to note perhaps for those that know me, that I wouldn't be who I am today without being shown the great compassion by some of the people that came into my life.

Without them reaching out to connect with me, who would I be?

Would I be a busker, writing songs and working on poetry books, having not had some inspiration and support from some others?
Or would I have slipped into a life of institutionalisation perhaps all my life living in hostels and even still begging out on the street?

If you've ever thought about fostering, and can provide not only a welcoming home but put in the time to connect with young people on an emotional level and basically just be a good friend, then I highly recommend it for those who feel that they have the patience.

Especially for those helping cases such as myself or even more challenging.

If you're young-at-heart, and willing to let those kids be a part of your natural everyday life, you'd probably be great for it.
Even in the children's homes it was those that would come and spend the time to chat and hang out with us from time to time, that would earn our greatest respect.

I would like to say a really big thanks to the staff at The Connections at St Martins day centre for their help in getting me off the streets at the age of sixteen, as well as the Centrepoint hostel they had referred me to afterwards.

A massive thanks to all my friends for their great support with helping me to make this book possible.

To Neil Paterson for his outstanding artwork for the book cover. You have been a massive help and I can't thank you enough.

To Matt, Chloe and the Yogurt Top Media team for their outstanding support with this book and helping to sponsor my first ever book run along with Caffe Del Nino's whom have also been fantastic.

All the creative clan at Nino's in Cannock, as well as the lovely folk in Hednesford's Woody's bar.

My dad and my sister, Kirsty, for their sound encouragement and support whilst writing this book.

My mum, for doing all she has and raising me to have

respect and care for others.

Kevin, for showing me another world that I may have never knew existed.
Virginia for being my teacher of wisdom into adulthood, Andres, and Oihana.
And Danielle for being a wonderful mum to my daughter.

Martin, Tracey, Pip, Mark, and Michelle amongst many others.

And Sylvie, for being the constant reminder that I'll always have something to fight and stay strong for.

Everyone else, you all know who you are.

I hope that you've enjoyed tagging along with me on some of my old adventures, from a lifetime ago.

Big Love
and
Bless.

www.BenWestwoodUK.blogspot.co.uk
Facebook.com/PoemsFromaRunaway
Twitter - @PoemsFaRunaway

MORE LINKS

The Connection at St Martins
https://www.connection-at-stmartins.org.uk/

The Dellow centre
http://www.providencerow.org.uk/

Centrepoint
https://centrepoint.org.uk/

Printed in Great Britain
by Amazon